ENDS APART

MALAYSIA AND KUWAIT

JASBIR S. JUGGI

CONTENTS

Part III
Pearls of Arabian Gulf

Part IV
Malaysia and Kuwait

PREFACE

In the 1960s and 1970s, India's highly educated academics faced limited career prospects and often sought opportunities abroad, particularly in English-speaking countries like the USA and UK. This trend attracted talented individuals from developing nations pursuing doctoral degrees in various fields. Despite focusing on higher education in their home countries, the lack of competitive salaries and working conditions often drove graduates to seek better opportunities elsewhere. Many well-educated graduates from renowned Indian universities began migrating overseas during this period.

In 1968, armed with a medical background and a PhD, I left India and embarked on a journey to explore new opportunities. I was offered a research position in Bethesda, USA, and an academic role at the newly established Medical Faculty in Kuala Lumpur, Malaysia. Opting for Malaysia, I spent twelve fulfilling years contributing to the country's development. Malaysia's stunning landscapes and vibrant culture provided ample personal and professional growth opportunities.

However, in the early 1980s, I received an enticing offer from the Faculty of Medicine at Kuwait University, promising better rewards and working conditions. Reluctantly leaving Malaysia, my family and I settled in Kuwait's arid desert landscape. The contrast between the two countries, not only in geography and climate but also in financial remuneration, became evident. I dedicated nearly three decades to service in Kuwait and briefly in Bahrain following the Gulf War in 1991. During this time, I explored the unique charm of Bahrain and other islands dotting the Arab Gulf Peninsula, meticulously documenting my experiences.

My travels and observations form the basis of the book "Ends Apart: Malaysia and Kuwait," which examines these two distinct regions. It delves into my encounters with the ethnic Peninsular Malay and Peninsular Arab Gulf populations, particularly the Kuwaiti people. Within its pages, I explore their histories, cultures, lifestyles, economies, working conditions, and attitudes towards expatriates, especially academics.

Part I

Malaysia: Peninsula Malaya

Chapter 1

PENINSULA MALAYS

Peninsula Malays are the dominant population group in Malaysia and have played a significant role in the country's political history. They occupy the Peninsula, divided into eleven states and two federal territories. Malaysia is a federal constitutional monarchy with a ceremonial head-of-state, a monarch. Hereditary sultans rule nine states of the Peninsula. The sultans took turns being monarchs, called 'Yang di Pertuan Agong,' for a five-year term. The capital, Kuala Lumpur, a federal territory in the Peninsula, is the seat of the country's elected Parliament and the central government of Malaysia. The Parliament is elected from Malaysia's west (peninsular) and East (Sabah and Sarawak) wings, separated by 400 miles of the South China Sea.

Figure 1.1. Malaysia (dark green) / ASEAN except for Malaysia (dark grey) (https://commons.wikimedia.org/wiki/File:Location_Malaysia_ASEAN.svg) by Wikipedia user 'ASDFGHJ'. This image is dedicated to the public domain.

Figure 1.2. Relief map of Peninsula Malaysia Geographic limits of the map: N: 7.602° N S: 0.209° N W: 108.885° E E: 119.441° E (https://commons.wikimedia.org/wiki/File:Location_map_Peninsula_Malaysia.png) by 'Maps-For-Free', modified by Dr. Blofeld. This image is licensed under CC BY 3.0 (https://creativecommons.org/licenses/by/3.0/deed.en.

The country is a melting pot of ethnicities with diverse cultures, languages, and religions. Therefore, ethnic groups contribute to various lifestyles, beliefs, and social values. In addition to the native Malays, the Peninsula gives succour to peoples of two prominent immigration groups, Chinese and South Asians. Out of the South Asians, South Indian Tamils are a dominant group, with a small fraction of North Indians, mostly Sikhs. According to the 2017 census (Encyclopedia Britannica), ethnic Malays constituted the majority group at 50%, Chinese at 22.4% and Indians at 6.7%. The remaining are other citizen groups, including the oldest inhabitants of the land, the *Orang Asli,* and non-citizens.

Figure 1.3. Kampung Laut Mosque (https://commons.wikimedia.org/wiki/File:Around-Kota-Bharu- (19).jpg) by Igor Laszlo. This image is licensed under CC BY-SA 3.0 (https://creativecommons.org/licenses/by-sa/3.0/).

'Kampung Laut Mosque in Tumpat, Kota Baru, is one of Malaysia's oldest mosques, dating from the 15ᵗʰ to early 18ᵗʰ century, and it was likely built in 1676. The Indian Hindu and Chinese Buddhist styles influence the architecture of the Mosque. The floor plan is square, and the roof is a three-tiered pyramid. The end ridge cap symbolizes a dragon. This early Malaysian mosque of the 17ᵗʰ century was devoid of traditional minarets, first introduced during the Abbasid rule in the Middle East in the 8ᵗʰ century. Four towers were added to Mecca's great mosque during the Abbasid rule. The tower behind the mosque may be the traditional minaret.'

The other immigrant group that settled was a small number of Arab traders from the Arab Peninsula. Arab traders have traded with the Malays on the Peninsula's West Coast since ancient times. With the emergence of Aden in Yemen as the major port of the Arab Peninsula, Arab traders came in large numbers, trading with coastal Malays on their way to China. Major trade picked up between the 12ᵗʰ and 15ᵗʰ centuries when Islam was introduced in Malaya. Port of Aden became an important gateway for the Arabs of the Hadramaut area of Yemen to migrate to Malay-speaking southeast Asian countries, including the Malay Peninsula. The initial settlers established themselves in the Pahang and Kelantan districts of the Eastern Peninsula, where, more than three hundred years old, one of the first mosques in the Peninsula, the *Kampong Laut mosque*, is located and has been maintained in good condition since. Later, they spread to Singapore and the mainland of the peninsula, particularly in the northern regions around Kuala Perlis. The Arab settlers, a well-defined group of a few hundred, settled in the late 19th century in British Singapore, in a Middle Road quarter bounded by Arab, Baghdad, Basrah, and Jeddah streets of those days. The Arabs who settled in the Peninsular, however, had no such defined settlement areas. They dispersed to the villages and became one with the native Malays, speaking their language and adopting their customs. The local Malays received the Arab settlers with great respect as they came from the holy land, were knowledgeable in Islamic religion, customs, and traditions, and were regarded as preachers. The Arabs also made inroads into the ruling Malay hierarchies of the Peninsula, some through marriage or otherwise adopted royal titles. The descendants of the Hadramaut Arabs today hold high political, administrative, business, and academic positions in Malaysia.

Malays owned the land (*Tanah Melayu*) . They preferred to stay with their land in the countryside, though several were migrating to cities for better lives, job opportunities, and their children's education. The majority of these Malays would live in the huts in the Kampongs (villages) spread in and around major cities, along with economically weak Indians and some Chinese. The City of Kuala Lumpur boasts several such Kampongs, the most prominent of which is in the city centre area called Kampong Baru (new village).

Most Malays in the countryside and cities dwell in longhouses. The longhouse is made up of piles, and its roof is usually a thatched roof called an atap woven from palm leaves, but most have corrugated iron sheets. Each longhouse contains several rooms or *bilek* where families live. Palm, banana, papaya, and other types of local fruit trees, including rambutan trees, surround the houses in the fertile lands of rural Malaya.

Figure 1.4. Cloudy Morning - Kampung Baru. (https://www.flickr.com/photos/naimfadil/15558481058/) by Naim Fadil. This image is licensed under CC BY SA 2.0 (https://creativecommons.org/licenses/by-sa/2.0/deed.en) 'Kampung Baru, Kuala Lumpur,Malaysia. Across the road from Kampong is New Kuala Lumpur, boasting high-rise buildings and the abode of the affluents.'

Figure 1.5. **Top:** An Old House of Kedah (https://www.flickr.com/photos/shazaphoto/3334750015/) by Flickr user '©Shaza79'. This image is licensed under CC BY 2.0 (https://creativecommons.org/licenses/by/2.0/deed.en#). **Bottom:** Photo Walk | Langkawi (https://www.flickr.com/photos/esharkj/5831490657/) by Flickr user 'esharkj'. This image is licensed under CC BY 2.0 (https://creativecommons.org/licenses/by/2.0/deed.en#)

Rice is the common crop grown, and some villages maintain cash crop plantations like palm oil and rubber trees. Coastal villagers indulge in fishing. Fertile land, frequent rainfall, and wild growth of fruit trees maintained the livelihood of rural Malays for centuries. Rural Malays were self-contained lots and did not venture out for innovations until the arrival of the 19th century CE.

Malays are generally quite gentle, reserved, and discreet people. They value courtesy, non-confrontation, and self-restraint. They dress modestly, typically speak politely and with gentle behaviour, and approach daily life with a great deal of patience, sometimes misunderstood as being indolent. In their society, such behaviour is considered refined (*halus*) and cultured (*budi Bahasa*). Malays are family-oriented people and often live in extended families. Ethnic Malays and Orang Asli are referred to as *Bumiputeras* (sons of the soil) to distinguish them from the immigrant communities labelled as *non-Bumiputeras*. Peninsular Malays speak a version of the Malay language, *Bhasha Malaysia,* which is now the country's official language. Malaysia's official religion is Islam, which all Malays profess. Like their co-religionists, Malays are fatalistic and attribute all misfortunes and failures in life to the will of God.

Since ancient times, Peninsular Malays came under Indian cultural and religious influences like the rest of Southeast Asia. South Indian Tamils made contact with the peninsular Malays almost 2000 years back.

The trade contacts thus established exposed the native Malays to the dominant religions of India, Hinduism and Buddhism. Indian religious, cultural, and economic values spread, Hindu monarchies were established, and the Sanskrit language started spreading in the Peninsula. Hindu temples began appearing, and the rulers were styled as Rajas. Several Hindu kingdoms existed, but the major one was Sirivijaya's kingdom. The Srivijayan era is considered the golden age of Malay culture, and the great port city of Malacca was established as the seat of Sirivijaya's kingdom. The Malay language was enriched with Sanskrit words, and Tamil culture penetrated the Malay society.

Figure 1.6. View of Masjid Negara from Kuala Lumpur Tower in 2023 (https://commons.wikimedia.org/wiki/File:Masjid_Negara_view_from_Kuala_Lumpur_Tow er_2023.jpg) by 'Pangalau.' This image is licensed under CC BY-SA 4.0 (https://creativecommons.org/licenses/by-sa/4.0/deed.en).

Islamic incursions into peninsular Malaya occurred between the 12th and 15th centuries through the Arab traders and later in the 15th century through the Indian Tamil Muslim traders when most of India was already under Islamic influence. South Indian Hindu Tamils lost influence in their southeast Asian colonies, the Malay peninsula, and Broneo came under Islam's sway. Malacca Sultanate was established, and Islam became the religion of both wings of Malaysia, Peninsular or West Malaysia, Borneo (Sabah and Sarawak) or East Malaysia. The Sultans of the states of peninsular Malaya patronized Islam, and the central government adopted it as the national religion of Malaysia. The Sankritised Malay language stayed, and South Indian cultural traditions were absorbed into the Islamic Malay society. The Malay language was also enriched with Arabic words.

Masjid Negara (National Mosque) was unveiled around my arrival in Kuala Lumpur. Located not far from the city centre area, the beautiful architectural design was the only of its kind in Southeast Asia. It is a small elegant mosque designed for 15000 worshipers.

Figure 1.7. Places of Worship in Kuala Lumpur. (https://commons. wikimedia.org/wiki/File:Places_of_worship_in_KL.png) compilation by Wikimedia user 'Junchuann.' This image is licensed under CC BY-SA 4.0 (https://creativecommons.org/licenses/by-sa/4.0/deed.en). **Upper Left**: The National Mosque in Kuala Lumpur, Malaysia (https://commons.wikimedia.org/wiki/File:Masjid_Negara_KL.JPG) by Wikimedia Commons User 'Niro5'; **Upper Right**: The Thean Hou temple in Kuala Lumpur (https://commons.wikimedia.org/wiki/File:Thean_Hou_KL_2007_pano_002.jpg) by Wikimedia Commons User 'Gryffindor'; **Lower Right**: The Sri Mahamariamman Temple (https://commons.wikimedia.org/wiki/File:Sri_Mahamariamman_Temple_2,_central_Kuala_Lumpur.jpg) by Wikimedia Commons User 'Two hundred per cent'; **Lower Left:** Cathedral of St. John The Evangelist at Jalan Bukit Nanas (https://commons.wikimedia.org/wiki/File:St._John%27s_Cathedral,_Kuala_Lumpur.jpg) by Wikimedia Commons User 'Two hundred per cent.'

There is religious freedom in the country; all the immigrant communities practice their religion freely and are permitted to raise their places of worship. Sometimes, the central government gives financial grants to construct religious places. Malays profess Islam and are very tolerant of the country's non-Islamic religions. Virtually all the world religions are represented in the country. On tours of cities of peninsular Malaysia, one will observe diverse ethnic people and their spectacular religious places of worship. Chinese temples are devoted to Buddhism, Confucianism, and Taoism, alongside Islamic worship places. Equally impressive are scores of Tamil Hindu temples in the cities that have spread all over the countryside, including the plantations since the early arrival of Tamil Hindu workers, who have been tilling the land in the plantations of Malaysia. So are the Christian Churches of various denominations. The Malays, by nature, are Pacific people and shun extremism, including religious extremism.

The religious co-existence is striking and is summed up in the Malaysian tourism promotion motto, *'Malaysia Truly Asia.'*

When I arrived in the country, most of the Malay population was in rural areas. The Islamic preachers in the village mosques were imparting religious education to their children within the limitations of their knowledge; with the urbanization of Malays, Islamic educational institutions developed in the cities, imparting religious education and other courses and enlightening the believers. A dedicated university offered science and professional courses, including Medicine and engineering. Higher education in Malays spread, and the graduates from these universities were involved for the first time in the nation-building processes.

Traditional rural-based society developed till the 18th century CE when Great Britain started colonizing the Malay peninsula and Borneo.

Malay culture has had ancient Indian roots for centuries, and its language is enriched with Sanskrit and Dravidian words. After the arrival of Islam in the 16th century CE, the Malay language and culture further developed on Arabic and Islamic traditions. However, the Indian roots of the language and cultural imprints on Malay social traditions, music, and dances are still present.

Malay music is mainly based on percussion instruments, the most important of which is the drum (*gendang or Kendang* in Malay).

Figure 1.8. **Top:** Sumazau Dance by PERSIS USM at Thaksin University (https://commons.wikimedia.org/wiki/File:Sumazau_dance_at_Thaksin_University.jpg) by Wikimedia user 'Athikhun. Suw'. This image is licensed under CC BY-SA 4.0 (https://creativecommons.org/licenses/by-sa/4.0/deed.en). **Bottom:** Young School Children Performing the Zapin Dance (https://www.flickr.com/photos/man/208928049/) by Airiz Norman. This image is licensed under CC BY-SA 2.0 (https://creativecommons.org/licenses/by-sa/2.0/).

Malay costumes have a large variety with or without *Batak floral* designs, particularly women's dresses, in different parts of the country. Malay women and men have many dress styles to choose from. There are traditional Early Styles of Baju Kurung and Baju Kebaya for the women, which are two pieces of clothes: the lower one is wrapped around the hip, covering the lower parts of the body and is called *kain sarong,* and the piece wrapped around the upper body is called *kain kanban.* The third piece is the head cloth called *kain kelubung.* Baju Kurung is now the formal dress of Malay women. Classical styles are preferred in Malacca, Johar Baru, and Kedah. During the sultanate of Malacca, Baju Melayu for men originated. This costume consisted of a long-sleeved shirt (baju) with a raised collar called a cekak musang collar and a round collar called a *teluk belanga* collar. The trouser is called *celana or seluar.* In formal attire, a skirt-type gilding or Sarong is added. Black round-head gear or *songkok* is worn to complete the traditional dress. This Malaccan-style dress remained in Malay society for hundreds of years and, with some modifications, is now Malaysia's national dress.

Baju Muskat, originally from ancient Muscat, Oman, is the modern style dress of the King of Malaysia, Yang di-Pertuan Agong, and is worn during the coronation ceremony.

Figure 1.9. **Left:** Bisaya Traditional Costume Right:(https://commons. wikimedia.org/wiki/File:Bisaya_Beaufort.jpg) by Wikimedia user 'Afgg97'. This image is licensed under CC BY-SA 4.0 (https://creativecommons.org/ licenses/by-sa/4.0/deed.en). **Right:** Women from Palembang in Ikat weave, (https://commons.wikimedia.org/wiki/File:Women_from_Palembang_in_ Ikat_weave,_Wanita_di_Indonesia_p29_(Ministry_of_Information.jpg) image taken from Women in Indonesia by Ch Sj Dt Tumenggung. This image is in the public domain.

The Sarong is a casual lower dress for men at home or outside. This simple dress is also used in Southeast Asian countries, South Asia, the Middle East, and Africa. Sarong is a long tubular cloth or just a length of cloth wrapped around the waist. It is a comfortable and airy casual wear made up of different types of fabrics, but mostly cotton cloth with flowery or batik designs. It is called *Lungi* in South Asia and *Izzar* in West Asia. Before the independence of India in 1947, lungi was commonly used in the Punjab countryside and other parts of India. However, after independence, its use was gradually reduced and replaced by Kurta-Pyjama (shirt-trouser), mainly made of cotton cloth. When I arrived in Kuala Lumpur, Sarong was commonly used in Malay and Indian homes. I also started wearing it at home.

Malay cuisine is the traditional food of the Malay communities of Southeast Asia. The dishes prepared are rich in spices and creamy coconut milk. Some popular dishes are nasi lemak, beef rendang, nasi himpit (rice cooked in palm leaves), Laksa (spicy noodles), spicy meat and vegetable curries, and satay.

Almost immediately after I joined my department at the university, one of the Malay subordinate staff invited the American head of the department and me for lunch during the Muslim festival of Eid at his Kampong house. Some of the dishes mentioned above were cooked and served by his wife and were delicious but spicy.

There were very few Malay food restaurants in Kuala Lumpur then, all run by Indonesians.

Chapter 2

IMMIGRANTS AND URBANIZATION

My association with Kuala Lumpur and Malaysia started in late 1968 when I sought better opportunities abroad after obtaining medical and doctoral qualifications from India. I was offered an academic position at the Faculty of Medicine at the University of Malaya, Kuala Lumpur, which I joined in Nov.1968.

Kuala Lumpur was a small city in the valley, bisected by two rivers, the confluence of which marked the city centre. The business areas of the city had Chinese-style shophouses. There were few high-rise buildings in the city centre area where Chinese and Indian businesses were located. The city had hectic business activity, and all three dominant communities operated within their spheres of interest.

Figure 2.1. Masjid Jamek along Klang & Gombak River (https://commons. wikimedia.org/wiki/File:Masjid_Jamek_along_Klang_%26_Gombak_Rive r_(220512)_06.jpg) by Wikimedia user 'angys'. This image is licensed under CC BY-SA 4.0 (https://creativecommons.org/licenses/by-sa/4.0/deed.en).

'The confluence of the Gombak (left) and Klang (right) rivers and Jamek Mosque in the centre. The earliest settlement of Kuala Lumpur was developed on the right side of the river. The image shows recent developments and landscaping.'

Figure 2.2. Section of a Panoramic View of Kuala Lumpur ca. 1884 (https://commons.wikimedia.org/wiki/File:Panorama_of_Kuala_Lumpur_ ca._1884.jpg) image taken from the book 'A Vision of the Past – A History of Early Photography in Singapore and Malaya. The photographs of G. R. Lambert & Co.'. This image is in the public domain.

'To the left is the Padang (Independence Square). The buildings were constructed of wood and atap before regulations enacted by Swettenham in 1884 required buildings to use bricks and tiles. The appearance of Kuala Lumpur transformed rapidly in the following years due to building regulations.'

Figure 2.3. Dataran Merdeka (Independence Square) in Kuala Lumpur, Malaysia (https://commons.wikimedia.org/wiki/File:Dataran_Merdeka_2.jpg) by Haakon S. Krohn. This image is licensed under CC BY-SA 3.0 (https://creativecommons.org/licenses/bysa/3.0/).

The buildings on the right of Padang (formerly Selangor Club) are ancient Moorish-style British colonial buildings used for government offices. The building is a landmark of Kuala Lumpur.

Figure 2.4. Guangzhou (formerly Canton) Chinese Boats (https://commons. wikimedia.org/wiki/File:Guangzhou,_Chinese_Boats_by_Lai_Afong,_ca_ 1880. jpg) by Lai Afong. This image is in the public domain.Chinese Junks in Victoria Harbor, Hongkong.

Chinese immigrants from southeastern China started coming to Borneo (East Malaysia) and peninsular Malaysia as early as the late 13th century CE. The available mode of sea transport was the *Junk*, a type of Chinese sailing ship with fully battened sails. The major migration groups started in the 16th century CE, mainly from the Chinese provinces of Fujian and Guandong. Immigration picked up during the Dutch occupation of the Peninsula in the 17th and 18th centuries CE. With the establishment of British settlements in the Malay islands of Penang in the north and Singapore in the south tip of the Peninsula during the 18th and 19th centuries CE,

Chinese immigrants from mainland China flooded the islands and the Peninsula. Tens of thousands of Chinese immigrants occupied the empty spaces on the islands of Penang and Singapore, coastal areas, and the mainland of the Peninsula.

The native Malays generally welcomed them since they brought exotic consumer goods from mainland China to sell. Singapore and Penang became almost exclusively Chinese-dominated islands. After Malaysia gained independence from Great Britain, Singapore was granted the status of a self-governing independent city-state. Singapore is now one of the world's most progressive and prosperous city-states.

Figure 2.5. Tin Mines at Kampar in Ipoh, Malaysia, around 1910. (https:// digitalcollections.universiteitleiden.nl/view/item/913144) by Kleingrothe, Carl Josef, sourced from Royal Netherlands Institute of Southeast Asian and Caribbean Studies and Leiden University Library/Wikimedia Commons. This image is in the public domain.

Early immigrants settled in small groups and developed a village-based agricultural economy. As immigration increased, the villages became small towns, and cities spread across peninsular Malaya. They diversified from an agri-based economy to business and later in tin mining activities. Tin ore has been mined in Malaysia for centuries. The methods used were primitive, and mining activities were confined along the river banks. However, commercial exploitation of tin mining occurred with the arrival of British colonizers when large deposits of ore were discovered by one Long Ja'afar in the northern Perak area and later in the Selangor area of the Peninsula in 1848.

Figure 2.6. Petaling Street, Kuala Lumpur, Malaysia (https://www.flickr.com/photos/139654283@N04/25978266001/) by Marcin Pieluzek. This image is licensed under CC BY 2.0 (https://creativecommons.org/licenses/by/2.0/deed.en#).

Malay chief Long Ja'afar employed Chinese miners to mine his land. Tin mining was lucrative, and the Chinese merchants invested in tin mining, which led to a further influx of Chinese immigrants. Chinese have become rich and diversified their resources to medium- and large-scale businesses. Disagreements between the Malay chiefs and their Chinese partners led to frequent conflicts requiring British intervention. The British brought in dredges, which increased tin production tremendously.

The Chinese controlled most of the trade and established almost complete financial control. They developed a banking system and provided a constant money supply for businesses and small-scale industries in peninsular Malaya. When I arrived in Kuala Lumpur in late 1968, the Chinese controlled 70-80% of the country's economy. They owned big and small businesses, banks, and city real estate. Chinese were the most affluent population group in the country. Almost all the top rich people were of Chinese origin, with few Indians and hardly any Malay. This pattern of the money distribution is still enduring today.

Recent statistics (Encyclopedia Britannica) indicate that seven out of ten top rich people in Malaysia today are Chinese, two are Indians, and one is Malay.

Chinese developed the cities in Malaya and expanded trade. They established exclusive Chinese-dominated commercial areas in the cities of the Peninsula called 'Chinatowns.' The capital city of Kuala Lumpur boasted the largest Chinatown, where, among other Chinese merchandise, all types of animal meat delicacies preferred by the Chinese were available. Such Chinatowns are also present in the world's cities where the Chinese have a sizable population. Malays and Chinese developed the cities in Malaya and expanded trade. They established exclusive Chinese-dominated commercial areas in the cities of the Peninsula. Malays made inroads into the city areas and started migrating in large numbers, swelling the ranks of kampongs. The older generation of Malays was primarily rural and attached to their land holdings and agriculture-based economy.

Urbanization started in earnest during the 19th and 20th centuries CE, with groups of Malays migrating and settling in cities. The younger generation of Malays, encouraged by the Malay-dominated central governments, were increasingly entering local universities for higher education. Educated Malays were filling government offices. In 1968, the recruits for Malaysian police and army came mainly from Malays, with some contributions from the Indian Sikh community and a few Chinese.

Educated Malays were appointed to government offices and occupied well-paid jobs in the ministries. Most Chinese were content with controlling businesses, big and small, as well as banking and money supply in the country.

Figure 2.7. Chinese Temples in Malaysia. **Upper Left:** Aerial view of Kek Lok Si at dusk (https://commons.wikimedia.org/wiki/File:Kek_Lok_Si_at_dusk.jpg) by Wikimedia user 'HundenvonPenang.' This image is licensed under CC BY-SA 4.0 (https://creativecommons.org/licenses/by-sa/4.0/de.).**Upper Right**: Yu Lung San Tien En Si (JadeDragonTemple)(https://commons.wikimedia.org/wiki/File:Chinese_style_temple_at_Jade_Dragon_Temple.jpg) by Wikimedia user 'Wingsancora93'. This image is licensed under CC BY-SA 4.0 (https://creativecommons.org/licenses/by-sa/4.0/deed.en).**Lower Left:** Sandakan, Sabah: Tam Kong Temple (https://commons.wikimedia.org/wiki/File:Sandakan_Sabah_Tam-Kong-Temple-01.jpg) photo by CEphoto, Uwe Aranas. This image is licensed under CC BY-SA 3.0 (https://creativecommons.org/licenses/by-sa/3.0/). **Lower Right**: Pagoda at Kek Look Seah Temple (https://commons.wikimedia.org/wiki/File:Pagoda_at_Kek_Look_Seah_Temple.jpg) by Wikimedia user 'Williamteoh97'. This image is licensed under CC BY-SA 3.0 (https://creativecommons.org/licenses/by-sa/3.0/).

'**Kek Lok Si Temple**, George Town, Penang. It is the largest Buddhist temple in Malaysia. I visited it during my visits to Penang. **Jade Dragon Temple**, Sibu, Sarawak, East Malaysia. The temple has places of worship for Buddhism, Confucianism and Taoism.**Tam Kung Temple**, Sabah, East Malaysia. The temple was established by Hakka Chinese immigrants in 1894. **Kek Look Seah Temple**, Ipoh, Perak. The temple is for the worship of Mahayana Buddhism.'

As I observed during my twelve-year stay in the country, Malaysian Chinese are enterprising, hard-working, and progressive people who generally exhibit remarkable resilience and diligence. They are proud people who prize their achievements and successes and sometimes tend to show arrogance. It may be explained by the traditional Chinese concept of '*Kiasu,*' in Chinese as '惊输 or 怕輸, meaning 'fear of losing.' This concept encourages competition to attain their goal and be ahead of others, promoting a queuing culture. Kiasu motivates the Chinese to achieve in everyday life, economically and academically. Kiasuism is ingrained into the Malaysian and Singapore Chinese at all levels of society and is a part of the traditional Chinese education system. Malaysian and Singaporean Chinese success stories are mainly built on this concept. Malaysian Chinese generally strive hard to achieve success and affluence. However, they keep their poise and do not display aggressive behaviour. Malaysian Chinese control almost 70% of the country's economy and are regarded as an astute, business-savvy ethnic group in Malaysia.

Most Malaysian Chinese people adhere to Buddhism; many practice Mahayana and some Theravada Buddhism. There are also a small number of Confucianists, Taoists, Christians, Muslims, and Hindus. They built appropriate religious places in different parts of the country to practice their adopted religion.

Chinese also contributed to the cultural life of Malaysia with their traditional music and dance, notably the Lion Dance. The lion dance is performed to bring good luck and fortune.

The lion dance is traditional in Chinese culture and other East and Southeast Asian countries, such as Tibet, Bhutan, and Sikkim. The performers wear lion costumes and mimic lion movements. The lion dance is performed during the Lunar New Year festivities, other Chinese and regional religious and cultural festivals, and the celebration of international events. Lion dances are an ancient tradition in China, from where they should have originated. Lion dance has been described in ancient Chinese texts where the wild beast and phoenix dances are mentioned, and these dances may have been masked performances. This dance transformed over the centuries in mainland China, and several regional versions now exist.

Figure 2.8. Lion Dance: **Right:** Múa lân trong lễ hội làng Triều Khúc (Lion Dance in Trieu Khuc Village Festival)(https://web.archive.org/web/20161023111016/http://www.panoramio.com/photo/69535514) by Vũ Hùng. This image is licensed under CC BY-SA 3.0 (https://creativecommons.org/licenses/by-sa/3.0/). **Left:** 日本語: 蜷城の獅子舞です。 (This is Ninashiro's lion dance) (https://commons.wikimedia.org/wiki/File:蜷城の獅子舞.JPG) by Naotake Naito (Wikimedia user '内藤 尚武'). This image is licensed under CC BY-SA 3.0 (https://creativecommons.org/licenses/by-sa/3.0/pl/deed.en). 'Right: **Hanoi**, Lion Dance at the Trieu Khuc village festival. Left: **Fukuoka**, Japan. Lion Dance of Minagi shrine in Asakura.'

Figure 2.9. Kinryū no mai (Golden Dragon Dance) of Sensō-ji (https://commons.wikimedia.org/wiki/File:Senso-ji_Kinryu-no-mai_02.jpg) by Wikimedia user 'Tak1701d'. This image is licensed under CC BY-SA 3.0 (https://creativecommons.org/licenses/by-sa/3.0/).

Dragon Dance is another ancient and traditional Chinese cultural dance performed during festive occasions. The dance is performed by experienced performers who manipulate a giant flexible puppet of a dragon using poles. The dancers simulate the unduteous, sinuous movements that seem to be going through the length of the dragon-like river waves. This dance is also described in ancient Chinese texts. The Chinese dragon was perceived to be associated with rain in ancient times. So, to appease the rain dragon deity during drought, this dance was performed. Nowadays, dance forms part of Chinese cultural dances and is performed during festivities in the streets and the bylanes of cities and towns to the accompaniment of music and the sound of gongs.

Figure 2.10. Green Dragon on the Petaling Street Entrance (https://www.flickr.com/photos/goosmurf/2138087930/) by Yun Huang Yong. This image is licensed under CC BY SA 2.0 (https://creativecommons.org/licenses/by-sa/2.0/deed.en).

Chinese cuisine is exotic and a delicacy in the food courts of the world's cities. Chinese restaurants serve various dishes from various regions of China. The trade mark Hakka noodles, Peking Duck, Cantonese cuisine, Shandong cuisine, Jiangsu cuisine, and Sichuan cuisine are some popular culinary preparations. Restaurants in Chinatown offer the best Chinese regional food dishes. Chinese food is popular worldwide; big and small towns are dotted with restaurants. In London alone, there are upwards of 1100 Chinese food restaurants.

Chinese food restaurants were opening up in the early sixties of the last century in major cities of India, offering an Indianised food version. Spicy food was served to attract Indian diners. Even the Chinese soups were spicy. Too many spices kill the authentic taste of the food, as I found out after tasting it on a visit to Delhi. The original Chinese food I tasted in Kuala Lumpur was delicious and had natural flavours. The city boasted several large and small Chinese food restaurants. Chinese people prefer to eat in restaurants rather than cook at home. The home-cooked food was considered expensive because of the several ingredients required to cook it. It was a surprise to see that Chinese restaurants with large seating capacities were usually full, particularly at lunchtime. Pork meat, the main ingredient of Chinese cooking, was freely available in the markets. Its sale, however, was segregated in the vegetable and meat markets. At one end of the market, Halal meat for Malays was sold, and on the other end of the market, pork meat for the Chinese and others was marketed. Bottled alcoholic drinks were freely available. The preferred drink of the Chinese is various brands of French Brandy. Alcohol was also served in the hotels, bars, and restaurants. When I arrived in Kuala Lumpur in 1968 to join an academic job at the Univesity of Malaya, alcoholic drinks and pork dishes were served to the academic staff at the university club on a part of the university campus.

Figure 2.11. **Left:** Rubber Trees in Malaysia (https://commons.wikimedia.org/wiki/File:Rubbertrees_malaysia.jpg) by Craig (Wikimedia user 'Pizzaboy1'). This image is in the public domain. **Right:** Rubber Tree in Malaysia. Collection of latex. (https://commons.wikimedia.org/wiki/File:Rubbertree_malaysia.jpg) by Craig (Wikimedia user 'Pizzaboy1'). This image is in the public domain.

The second largest immigrant group of South Indians was implanted in the Peninsula by the British colonial rulers during the mid-19th to the mid-20th centuries. With the British acquisition of Penang, Malacca, and Singapore, also addressed as the Straits Settlements, from 1786 to 1824, the immigration of Indian labour from British India started in earnest. It included police officers, colonial soldiers (sepoys), traders, and plantation workers. Also, there was the migration of educated caders with a good command of English to work in the British colonial government of Straits Settlement.

To develop the cash crops in Peninsular Malaya and improve the economy, British colonists obtained rubber saplings from Brazil and transplanted them in Singapore in 1877. After that, rubber plantations were developed on a large scale in Peninsular Malaya with encouraging results. The mass plantation labour force was recruited from British India during the 19th and early 20th centuries, and South Indian Tamils constituted the primary group, making up almost 80%. The remaining were Malayalis, Telugu, and Bengalis from east India. They were hired under the *Indenture Kangani (headman) system, which is* characterized as "a new system of slavery" where a person is contracted without salary for a specific number of years (Viswanathan,2021). Bumper rubber harvests were produced. Rubber became the primary export commodity from British colonial Malaysia, and by the 1930s, peninsular Malaya produced half of the world's natural rubber. I visited the rubber plantations around Kuala Lumpur, and it was fascinating to see the milky latex oozing out from a carefully placed cut in the stem of the rubber tree.

The other cash crop planted by the British was palm oil. The palms were brought to Malaya from West Africa in 1870. Initially, they were grown as ornamental plants;

the oil potential of the plant was exploited in 1917 when official commercial planting took place. Indentured Indian labour was used to raise palm oil plantations in peninsular Malaya.

Britishers and other Europeans owned rubber and palm oil plantations. The local Malays hardly benefitted from these plantations.

Deeply embedded in traditions and religious beliefs, most Hindu Tamils started working in the plantations while preserving their spiritual, social, and cultural traditions. After completing the mandatory Kangani system, many relocated to the cities, swelling the spaces of Kampongs. They worked odd jobs and educated their children in better schools. Many of these children found places in professional education institutions in India, were self-supported, or were on scholarships. City-

Figure 2.12. Oil Palms in Malaysia (https://commons.wikimedia.org/wiki/File:Oilpalm_malaysia.jpg) by Craig (Wikimedia user 'Pizzaboy1'). This image is in the public domain.

dwelling children of police officers, colonial soldiers, traders, and office workers also received higher education from Indian universities. Upon return, medical and engineering degree holders found jobs in the respective ministries. Others found jobs in government offices and the education ministry.

Many Indians are also involved in business and trade. Most privately owned Indian businesses belonged to Tamil Chettiars, who doubled up as money lenders. North Indian Punjabis, particularly Sikhs, also own private businesses. The British recruited Sikhs to serve in the police and armed forces. They remained so till 1970 when the new economic policies were introduced favouring Malays, who now dominate these services.

Impressed by the marshal qualities of the Sikhs during the Anglo-Sikh wars of 1849, British colonial rulers brought Sikh police forces and sepoys from India to maintain law and order in their Southeast Asian colonies, Hong Kong and mainland China. However, their children, as with other Indians, were trained in India as doctors, engineers, lawyers, and accountants and, upon return, found jobs in the respective ministries.

When I arrived in Malaysia in 1968, the country's health sector was run mainly by Malaysian Indian doctors with a significant number of Sikh doctors, and so was the case with engineers, lawyers, and accountants.

Indians formed a significant part of the professional classes in Malaysia. However, this was changed in subsequent years due to the government's new economic policies grossly favouring the Malays. In 1990, Malaysian Indians represented only 15.5% of Malaysia's professional services. Although the Indian plantation workforce had reduced, many were still below the poverty line.

Figure 2.13. **Left:** Sri Poyyatha Vinayagar Moorthi Temple, in Malacca's Jln. Tokong (https://commons.wikimedia.org/wiki/File:Sri-Poyyatha-Vinayagar-Moorthi-Temple2205.jpg) by Vladimir Menkov. This image is licensed under CC BY-SA 3.0 (https://creativecommons.org/licenses/by-sa/3.0/). **Right:** A Hindu Temple Beside the Bird Park (https://flickr.com/photos/77742560@N06/12340299965) by Flickr user 'Shankar S.' This image is licensed under CC BY 2.0 (https://creativecommons.org/licenses/by/2.0/deed.en#).

'South Indian Hindu Temples in Malaysia.Gopuram of Sri Vinpper Ayagar Moorthi Temple, Malacca. The temple is dedicated to the elephant deity Vinayaga, also worshipped as Lord Ganesha. The elephant deity is the God of wisdom. The temple was raised in 1780 during the Duch rule and is the oldest Hindu temple in Malaysia. Arulmigu Karumariamman Temple, beside the Bird Park, Penang. The temple is dedicated to the Hindu deity Arulmigu Karumariamman, a mother deity worshipped by plantation workers. The temple has the largest gopuram in Malaysia and is 100 years old.'

Figure 2.14. **Right:** Batu Caves, 2022 (https://commons.wikimedia.org/wiki/File:Batu_Caves_stairs_2022- 05. jpg) by Wikimedia user 'Chainwit.'. This image is licensed under CC BY-SA 4.0 (https://creativecommons.org/licenses/by-sa/4.0/deed.en). **Left:** The Nagarathar Sivan Temple, Penang, in January 2019 (https://commons.wikimedia.org/wiki/File:Cmglee_Penang_Nagarathar_Sivan_Temple.jpg) by Wikimedia Commons User 'Cmglee.' This image is licensed under CC BY-SA 4.0 (https://creativecommons.org/licenses/by-sa/4.0/).

'*Batu Caves Hindu Temple Complex,* near Kuala Lumpur. The temple was founded in 1890 and is dedicated to Murugam, the Hindu God of war. The Tamil festival of Thaipusan is celebrated in this cave temple during January/early February. *Nagarathar Sivan Temple, Penang.* It was built in 1854 by the Chettiar community of Penang. The temple is dedicated to Lord Shiva, known as The Destroyer within the trimurthy (Hindu Trinity), which includes Brahma and Vishnu. Shiva also creates and protects.'

Almost all South Asian religions are represented in the ethnic cauldron of Malaysia. But Hinduism is professed by the majority of Indo-Malaysian Tamils. They introduced the South Indian architectural design of Hindu temples in peninsular Malaya. The oldest Hindu temple, Sri Potha Moorthi Temple, is located in Malacca and was raised by the Tamil Chitty family during the Dutch colonial government of Malaya in 1780. Subsequent generations of Tamils created exquisitely designed, carved, chiselled, and crafted temples, stone, and marble images of Hindu deities. Because of their majestic architecture, they are very visible in the cities and countryside of Malaysia. The architectural design of the temples is hundreds of years old and is based on the architecture treatise Manasara Shilpa Shashtra, written several centuries back by the South Indian seer Manasara.

Tamils introduced the rich musical heritage of South India into Malaysia. Several classical dances of different genres are performed to the tune of various ragas (melody and rhythm). The dancer translates the rhythm of the played ragas with the movements of the eyes, face, arms, fingers, and legs. The classical dances performed include Bharatanatyam, Kathakali, Kucipudi, Sattriya, Manipuri Mohiniyattam, and the display of Nataraja. In Kuala Lumpur, there are schools run by the Tamil community where young girls are trained in South Indian musical art. My school-going daughters were also taught in one such school.

Figure 2.15. **Left:** A Bharatanatyam Dancer (https://commons.wikimedia. org/wiki/File:Bharata_Natyam_Performance_DS.jpg) by Augustus Binu. This image is licensed under CC BY-SA 3.0 (https://creativecommons. org/licenses/by-sa/3.0/). Middle: KathaKali Copyright © 2015 Prathyush Thomas (https://commons.wikimedia.org/wiki/File:Kathakali_BNC.jpg). Permission is granted to copy, distribute, and or modify this document under the terms of the GNU Free Documentation License, Version 1.2 or any later version published by the Free Software Foundation (https://www.gnu.org/ licenses/old-licenses/fdl-1.2.en.html#SEC1); with no 39 Invariant Sections, no Front-Cover Texts, and no Back-Cover Texts. A copy of this license is included in the section entitled "GNU Free Documentation License." **Right:** Photograph of Shiva as the Lord of Dance (https://collections.lacma.org/ node/240893) captured by Los Angeles County Museum of Art (LACMA), retouched by Julia W. This image is in the public domain.

The other ethnic groups of Indo-Malaysians include Malayallees, Telugus, and Punjabis. Sikhs are the dominant community among the Punjabis, and their number in Malaysia is around 100,000. First Sikhs to arrive in Malaya were political prisoners after the defeat of the Khalsa army in the Anglo-Sikh wars of 1849 and the loss of the Sikh empire of Punjab. They were Bhai

Maharaj Singh and Khurruck Singh. They were deported from Punjab due to anti-British activities.

Regular Sikh immigration to Malaya started in 1873. Impressed by their martial qualities during the Anglo-Sikh wars, increasing numbers of Sikhs were recruited into the British Indian armed forces. At the time of independence in 1947, Sikhs comprised 33% of the Indian army, even though they comprised 1.7% of the population of India. Sikhs also dominated the British police force in Punjab. The Sikh police force and Sepoys were sent to Malaya to maintain law and order, particularly in the northern tin mining areas, to control the warring Chinese gangs. After retirement, most stayed in Malaysia and became security guards and money lenders. Their children were educated in Indian and Australian universities, and upon return, they were appointed doctors, engineers, lawyers, and accountants in the government service.

Like other immigrant communities, Sikhs established their places of worship and cultural centres. The first Sikh gurdwara was founded in 1873 in the police lines by the Sikh police in Fort Cornwallis, Penang. The first public Gurdwara was set up in Penang in 1903. After that, several public gurdwaras appeared in all the cities and towns of West and East Malaysia. There are more than 119 gurdwaras in Malaysia. The city of Kuala Lumpur has 15 gurdwaras, more than the number of mosques, despite more Muslim residents in the city than Sikhs. The largest number of Gurdwaras,42, is located in the northern state of Perak, with Ipoh as its capital.

Indian cuisine has worldwide ramifications and is a preferred ethnic food enjoyed by millions worldwide. In the city of London, a staggering 8000 restaurants are serving Indian food delicacies compared to 1100 Chinese food restaurants. Indian cuisine has the second most Michelin Stars in the city, second only to French cuisine. Indian spicy curries, Biryanis, Naans, and Kebabs have flavours and tastes on which most dinners would get hooked. Although the food is generalized as Indian, household recipes created signature dishes. Butter chicken, chicken tikka masala, dal makhani, and tandoori (earthen oven) cooked chicken and kebabs are the preferred foods by gourmets worldwide. World leaders and celebrities visiting India especially look for these signature dishes on the menus.

Figure 2.16. **Upper Left**: Kuala Lumpur Gurdwara Sahib Police (https://commons.wikimedia.org/wiki/File:Kuala_Lumpur_Gurdwara_Sahib_Police.jpg) by Wikimedia User 'StagiaireMGIMO.' This image is licensed under CC BY-SA 4.0 (https://creativecommons.org/licenses/by-sa/4.0/deed.en). **Upper Right:** : Gurdwara Sahib Butterworth, Central Seberang Perai, Penang, Malaysia(https://commons.wikimedia.org/wiki/File:Gurdwara_Sahib_Butterworth.jpg) by Wikimedia User 'Chongkian.' This image is licensed under CC BY-SA 4.0 (https://creativecommons.org/licenses/by-sa/4.0/deed.en). Lower: Gurdwara Sahib Johor Baru, Johor Baru, Johor, Malaysia(https://commons.wikimedia.org/wiki/File:Gurdwara_Sahib_Johor_Baru.jpg) by Wikimedia User 'Chongkian.' This image is licensed under CC BY-Sa4.0(https://creativecommons.org/licenses/by-sa/4.0/deed.en.).

'Gurdwaras in Malaysia. ***Kuala Lumpur.*** The iconic Gurdwara was the first Gurdwara in the city and was built in the Police lines by the Sikh police personnel stationed there in 1898. ***Butterworth,*** Penang. Sikh security guards of the Straits Trading Company used a makeshift Gurdwara on the company premises in 1920. After their retirement, they built the present building of the Gurdwara in 1934. ***Johor Baru.*** In 1916, Sikh police officers serving in the Johar's Sultan guards requested that the commissioner grant them land to build a Gurdwara. The land was duly given, and Sikhs built the Gurdwara in 1921.'

However, when I arrived in Malaysia in the late sixties of the last century, the restaurant food culture for newly arrived Indians was just beginning. There were very few Indian food restaurants in Kuala Lumpur, and the best ones were in the starred hotels. On visits to Indian restaurants, it was rare to see Malay or Chinese diners. Malays, because of their religious injunction, will not eat food cooked in unclean places. The kitchen was considered unclean if pork meat was cooked. At the same time, Indians relish Chinese food. The restaurant food eating culture was deeply entrenched in the Malaysian Chinese. Chinese generally do not like spicy curries, but they would be comfortable eating them if offered. Chinese and Indian food traditions are centuries old and evolve new recipes from within, not necessarily imported from other cultures.

Tamil food traditions are centuries old; they do not have to innovate and borrow ideas from other cultures while preparing dosa-idli-sambar and several types of curries, their staple food. There were exclusive Tamil food restaurants and eateries where Tamil food delicacies could be enjoyed. Sikhs and other northern Indians patronized Punjabi food restaurants, and Punjabi signature dishes were served. Malay and Chinese diets are mainly rice-based, whereas wheat-based tandoori roti (bread) and nanns were staples to northern Indians.

Four prominent religious and cultural identities constitute the Malaysian cauldron of cultures. Each culture maintains a separate religious identity prescribed according to the tenets of its religion. Malay religion, Islam, is one of the Abrahamic religions and is monotheistic, and so is the Sikh religion. Christianity, an Abrahamic religion deemed monotheistic like other Abrahamic religions, firmly believes in the Holy Trinity, deeply ingrained in Christian thought. In contrast, Chinese and Tamil Hindu religions are polytheistic and firmly adhere to idol worship, anathema to Islam. Despite these religious contradictions, all three dominant ethnic communities maintain perfect peace and respect each other's religious identities. Malays are very tolerant, adaptive, and resilient people, and the Malay-dominated governments support the non-Muslim religious minorities and provide them with funds and land to build their holy places. A glaring example is more than 100 Sikh Gurdwaras (temples) in Malaysia for a total Sikh population of 100,000.

Notwithstanding the religious harmony, the main problem faced by the country is racial harmony. When I arrived in Kuala Lumpur in the late sixties of the last century, on the surface, I perceived perfect racial harmony. Still, it betrayed undercurrents of significant differences between the three dominant communities, mainly perceived on economic grounds and wealth distribution between the communities. It was the cause of severe racial turmoil that I witnessed when I was only six months into the country. These riots were severe enough to change the whole dynamics of the ethnic communities and radical political decisions were imposed, which granted unlimited benefits to Malays in an attempt to redistribute the wealth of the country and alleviate the economic ambitions of the restless Malay community.

Chapter 3

RACIAL RIOTS AND THEIR AFTERMATH

Racial integration in the multicultural society of Malaysia remained elusive. Several factors contribute to it. The three significant communities inhabiting Malaysia could not become homogenous because of inherent contradictions among them. The ethnic background of the communities was vastly different. Their religious background is different, their culture is diverse, and their economic aspirations vary in quality and quantity. During the British colonial period, the native Malays were left to their devices as an agricultural society with little encouragement to diversify and improve their lot. Higher education was mainly inaccessible to them, and their children followed the rural agricultural-based economy of their forefathers. Instead of encouraging the rural Malays to come out of their traditional working style and diversify in business, trade, and natural resource exploitation, the British rulers imported Chinese from mainland China to develop business and trade and exploit the country's mineral resources. They brought indentured Indian labour to plant and till the cash crops of rubber and palm oil. Native Malays and other indigenous people were left in slumber to mend for themselves. In due course, enterprising Chinese explored the mineral resources, developed tin mining industries, and virtually monopolized commerce and trade in the country. Chinese became economically affluent, with Malays gradually slipping into poverty. They lost their intrinsic drive to improve and develop economically. They could not move with time to evolve to a better horizon. Their slumber of decades cost them grit and determination, and they became fatalistic. At the time of the independence from British rule in 1957, 64.8% of Malays were below the poverty line compared to 26% of Chinese and 39.2% of Indians. The same figures in 1970, a year after the riots and 13 years after independence and constitutional guarantees of special rights to the Malays, were 73.61 % Malays, 18.11% Chinese, and 7.15% Indians, according to the figures issued by the Department of Statistics of Malaysia (Ravallion, Martin, 2020). Malay poverty increased during the first 13 years of independence, while the poverty of the other two ethnic groups was significantly reduced. This state of affairs occurred despite Malay being granted special status and special powers guaranteed in the country's first Constitution, proclaimed immediately after independence in 1957, which assured Malay supremacy.

After independence, Malaysia was ruled by a coalition of three ethnic groups represented by their respective mainstream political parties: United Malay National Organisation (UMNO), the Malaysian Chinese Association (MCA), and Malaysian Indian Congress (MIC), the ruling Troika of Malaysia. The coalition, initially called Alliance but later after the 1969 riots was renamed Barisan Nasional (National Coalition), agreed on the broad principles for sharing power: Malays were to hold political dominance, the Chinese were to control the country's economic sectors, and Indians were to play a lesser economic role. UMNO nominated Tunku Abdul Rahman as the first prime minister of independent Malaysia.

Tunku Abdul Rahman, a scion of the Kedah royal family, was a statesman and a lawyer who supervised the independence (Merdeka) from British colonial rule in 1957. He successfully incorporated British North Borneo, now Sabah and Sarawak, into Malaya to establish a larger entity of Malaysia. Tunku remained at the helm of the country's political affairs for thirteen years when he was forced to resign after the riots of 1969. However, he remained a respected statesman and is regarded as the architect of independence and founding father of Malaysia. His positive achievement was the incorporation of Sabah and Sarawak into Malaysia. Still, as seen by his distractors, his negative achievement was the expulsion of Singapore from Malaysia in 1965 to lessen the tensions between the Malay and the Chinese communities. More importantly, he failed to improve the economic status of Malays, who became poorer during his long rule. The financial indicators pointed out that since independence in 1957, Malay has become poorer and the Chinese richer. Mass discontent among Malays caused rumblings among a section of the UMNO patronized by the deputy prime minister Tun Abdul Razak. This section of Malays pressured the prime minister to grant Affirmative Action status to Bumiputras (Malays) and a 30% equity share of the national wealth. Tunku Abdul Rahman was not in favour of this, and he had his reasons to deny it. The radicals in UMNO were not amused by the position taken by the prime minister and became restive. Events in 1969 were moving fast, which precipitated racial riots in the city of Kuala Lumpur.

Figure 3.1. Aankomst Prins Abdoel Rahman op Ypenburg (Arrival of Prince AbdulRahmanatYpenburg)(https://www.nationaalarchief.nl/onderzoeken/fotocollectie/a9c0d8e6-d0b4-102d-bcf8-003048976d84) captured by Harry Pot / Anefo, sourced from DutchNational Archives. This image is dedicated to the public domainunderCC01.0.(https://creativecommons.

org/publicdomain/zero/1.0/?ref=chooser-v1). Portrait of Tunku Abdul Rahman, first Prime Minister of Malaysia

May 13, 1969, is the date in Malaysian history when the hell broke loose and communal riots started in earnest in the city of Kuala Lumpur, spilling over to Singapore. It was a violent outbreak of Sino-Malay sectarian tensions in the city of Kuala Lumpur following the 1969 general elections. The elections were peaceful, but the results triggered the clashes which followed. For the first time, the ruling coalition Alliance party received less than 50% of the share of votes and a reduced majority. Two main opposition parties, DAP (Democratic Action Party), a centre-left party, and Parti Gerakan, a liberal party dominated by the Chinese, made significant gains. Victory processions were paraded in the streets of Kuala Lumpur by the opposition parties using provocative slogans and epithets. It was seen as an attack on Malay power and supremacy, jeopardizing the future of Malay rule. Urgent action, therefore, was required to stop this tide. Malays also held their heads high and took out a victory parade. Prime Minister Tunku Abdul Rahman supported this decision by saying, "Retaliatory parade was inevitable as otherwise the UMNO party members would be demoralized after the show of strength by the Opposition and the insults that have been thrown at them."

Figure 3.2. **Upper Left:** KampongBharu(https://commons.wikimedia. org/wiki/File:Jalan_Raja_Muda_Musa,_Kampong_Bharu_(220813). jpg) By Wikimedia User 'angys.' This image is licensed under CC BY-SA 4.0 (https://creativecommons.org/licenses/by-sa/4.0/deed.en). **Upper Right:** ChowKit,KualaLumpur(https://commons.wikimedia.org/wiki/File:Jalan_Tuanku_Abdul_Rahman,_Kuala_Lumpur_20230813_123218. jpg) captured by Wikimedia User 'Wiki Farazi.' This image is dedicated to the public domain under CC0 1.0(https://creativecommons.org/publicdomain/zero/1.0/?ref=chooser-v1). Lower Left: Changkat Tunku, Bukit Tunku, KennyHills. (https://commons.wikimedia.org/wiki/File:Night_in_Kuala_Lumpur_(230517).jpg) by Wikimedia User 'angles'. This image is licensed under CC BY-SA 4.0(https://creativecommons.org/licenses/by-sa/4.0/deed.en).

The fateful procession of Malays started at 6.30 pm on Tuesday, May 13, 1969, from the edge of Kampong Baru, near the residence of Selangor Chief Minister Dato Harun, the rallying point. People started collecting there in the morning, and most came from outlying areas and far-off places since Kuala Lumpur city was predominantly Chinese. Some of them were attacked as they were passing through Chinese regions. When the news reached the mob at the chief minister's house around 6.30 pm, groups of Malays armed with parangs (large knives) and kris (daggers) fanned out to attack the Chinese in the surrounding and far areas of the city, spreading mayhem, killing, looting and burning Chinese properties. Chinese had contingency plans but were taken by surprise by the suddenness of the attack. Chinese recovered from the initial shock, and they retaliated using armed gang members of the Chinese secret societies. Malays were attacked wherever they were found in the Chinese areas, and their properties were burned. Chinese also tried to attack UMNO headquarters located on Batu Road and even surrounded a police station. Police took action later in the evening using tear gas, and a 24-hour- curfew was announced at 7.30 pm for the city of Kuala Lumpur. Shoot-to-kill orders were given at 9 pm. The army was deployed and reinforced the shoot-to-kill order. Hospitals, mortuaries, and emergencies were receiving killed and wounded Chinese and Malays. Most of the casualties occurred on 13th May night and 14th May morning, but killing, looting, and arson attacks continued for the next two days, and Chinese bodies with bullet wounds started appearing.

When the fury subsided after four days, counting of the spoils began. According to official sources, 160 people died, most of them Chinese. However, estimates from international sources and observers suggested a toll of 600. Hundreds of properties were burnt, and a few thousand people were made homeless. On May 14, a curfew was declared in the whole of the state of Selangor, and on May 16, a state of emergency was declared in the whole of the country; Parliament was suspended and replaced by a National Operations Council (NOC) headed by the deputy prime minister, Tun Abdul Razak.

I joined the Faculty of Medicine, University of Malaya, on November 1, 1968. I was newly married, and my wife, a captain in the Indian Army Medical Corp, accompanied me on a one-month holiday. She went back to complete the mandatory army service for another year. I lived alone and only six months into the country when this mayhem broke out. I was keeping abreast of all the political developments in the city. During my short stay, I made friends with a few well-placed Sikh families in the city, some of whom were known to me from India. Around May 10, my friend, a deputy general manager of Malaysian Railways, told me that the situation was critical and that I should shift to his house, which is much safer. He was staying in a big bungalow house, his official residence, at the posh residential area of Kenny Hills, now Bukit Tunku (Royal Hill). Kenny Hill has bungalow houses for high-ranking government officers and a high-class residential area for affluent people. Most homes are perched on low hills. The prime minister's residence was also located at the tallest hill facing the city centre of Kuala Lumpur. I shifted to my friend's house on the same day to await developments in the city. My friend was well-connected and would update me with the latest news.

When the full story of the riots unfolded on May 14, I was much agitated and apprehensive about my future in the country. However, my friend put me at ease by telling me that minor racial conflicts have been happening since the independence in 1957 when the Constitution was implemented, providing special status to Malays. The only other sizable racial conflict occurred in 1964 in Singapore, with a spillover in Kuala Lumpur, with some loss of life and property. But the situation was controlled, and normalcy was restored. He admitted that the present conflict was much more severe than ever since independence. He was confident that this conflict would also be controlled and that everyday life would return soon.

After a week, the curfew was lifted for a few hours so that people could buy food and other essential items. Provision stores were permitted to open. My friend escorted me and followed my car to my flat at the university campus, located at the junction of Kuala Lumpur and the satellite city of Petaling Jaya, 10 Km away. Military checkpoints were on the way, but they did not bother us. I visited the nearby Petaling Jaya market to shore up my food supplies. Teaching was resumed at the university after the daytime curfew was lifted. Sporadic incidents of killing, looting, and arson were still reported, mainly from Kampongs located in Kuala Lumpur. Complete normalcy was achieved by July 31, 1969.

The National Operations Council (NOC) went into action and defined and drafted the goals of the New Economic Policy (NEP) to alleviate Malay poverty and to uplift their economic status by redistribution of national wealth. The goal was to increase the ownership of enterprise by Bumiputras from the current 2.4 % to 30% share of the national wealth, which was earlier denied to them by Prime Minister Tunku Abdul Rahman. This policy was implemented.

After the emergency was lifted, the Constitution was restored, and Parliament reconvened on September 20, 1970, when Tunku Abdul Rahman resigned. Tun Abdul Razak took over as Prime Minister of Malaysia.

The next twelve years of my stay in Kuala Lumpur were spent in a relatively peaceful environment.

Chapter 4

UNIVERSITI MALAYA: FAKULTI PERUBATAN

The British colonial government of Malaya established the King Edward College of Medicine in Singapore in 1905, serving as the University Malaya's predecessor. The merger of the Raffles College and King Edwards College of Medicine in 1949 created the university in Singapore. Two autonomous university divisions were organized in 1959, one for Singapore and the other for Kuala Lumpur. After the independence of Singapore in 1964, the Singapore branch became the National University of Singapore, a renowned university in the world today. The second branch retained its original name, the University of Malaya, and the government of Malaya regularized it by legislation in 1961. It became the University of Malaya, Kuala Lumpur. The university has thirteen faculties, two academies, five institutes, and six academic centres.

Figure 4.1. Left: Copyright © 2010 Wikipedia User 'Lpsoldier007' (https://commons.wikimedia.org/wiki/File:Gambar_Dewan_Tunku_Canselor,_Universiti_Malaya.jpg). Permission is granted to copy, distribute, and/or modify this document under the terms of the GNU Free Documentation License, Version 1.2, or any later version published by the Free Software Foundation. (https://www.gnu.org/licenses/old-licenses/fdl-1.2.en.html#SEC1); with no Invariant Sections, no Front-Cover Texts, and no Back-Cover Texts. A copy of this license is included in the section entitled "GNU Free Documentation License." Right: Universiti Malaya KL Gate (https://commons.wikimedia.org/wiki/File:Universiti_Malaya_KL_gate.jpg) by Wikimedia User 'angys.' This image is licensed under CC BY-SA 4.0 (https://creativecommons.org/licenses/by-sa/4.0/deed.en).

The university is located in the picturesque Pantai Valley, at the border between Kuala Lumpur and its satellite city, Petaling Jaya. In the centre of the valley is a small lake fed by a creek. Various faculties and colleges of the university and university administration are located on the hills surrounding the valley. The academic staff's residences are located on either side of Jalan University (university road), part of Petaling Jaya, where one of the entrance gates of the university is also located. The entrance to the university hospital is also from this road.

Figure 4.2. Faculty of Medicine and University Hospital, University Malaya, Kuala Lumpur. The small building on the far left is the entrance to the faculty from the Pantai Valley campus of the university. This entrance I used to come to the faculty for 12 years. On top of it are offices of the Dean and faculty administration. The following four parallel blocks of buildings, four stories each, housed the preclinical and paraclinical departments, student laboratories, library, main auditorium, and lecture halls, among other teaching facilities. Then, there is the 12-story tower block housing the University Hospital, which was connected to the preclinical block by a passage. On the back of the tower are maternity and pediatric hospitals facing the main highway, the Federal Highway.

The Faculty of Medicine (Fakulti Perubatan), University of Malaya, was established in 1963, immediately after the inauguration of the University Malaya. The parent institution of the faculty was the 1905 King Edwards VII Medical School, based in Singapore, British Malaya. Dr T.J. Danaraj, a Malaysian of South Indian descent with more than 20 years of experience in medical education, was appointed as Professor of Medicine and founding Dean of the Faculty in 1963. His mandate was to develop a faculty par excellence with unlimited resources. A five-year course of medical studies was planned for the 100 students' intake per year. Prospective high school leavers were admitted after completing a two-semester premedical course at the Science Faculty.

The first batch of 64 students was admitted in 1964. The conventional Systems-based teaching module was adopted for the pre and para-clinical departments. The academic staff was accordingly recruited.

The pre- and para-clinical departments were built in 1965. The university hospital building was completed in 1968 when I joined the faculty of Medicine. The hospital, an imposing twelve-story building, became partly operational for teaching in 1967 and fully functional by 1968 Since hardly any qualified academics were available in the country, the teaching staff was recruited from abroad, notably Singapore, Australia, the UK, India, Sri Lanka, and Canada. China Medical Board of USA assisted in providing academic staff for various departments and equipment to furnish the student and research laboratories. The academic staff were mostly senior or retired professors from American universities. China Medical Board was an affiliate of the Rockefeller Association of the USA and assisted the newly established medical schools in China and Southeast Asia. When I joined the Department of Physiology, I was pleasantly surprised to see the academic staff's research laboratories equipped with the latest state-of-the-art research equipment.

Figure 4.3. **Upper Left:** Faculty of Medicine Beside the Faculty of Pharmacy (https://commons.wikimedia.org/wiki/File:Faculty_of_medicine_beside_the_faculty_of_pharmacy.jpg) by Wikimedia user 'Cerevisae.' This image is licensed under CC BY-SA 4.0 (https://creativecommons.org/licenses/by-sa/4.0/deed.en). **Upper Right:** The Main Tower of UMMC (https://commons.wikimedia.org/wiki/File:Pusat_Perubatan_Universiti_Malaya.jpg) by Wikimedia user 'Hidayat. Ismail. This image is licensed under CC BY-SA 4.0 (https://creativecommons.org/licenses/by-sa/4.0/deed.en). **Lower Left:** UMSC Specialist Outpatient Clinic (https://commons.wikimedia.org/wiki/File:UM_Specialist_Centre_(Outpatient_Clinic).jpg) by Wikimedia user 'Izwanos92'. This image is licensed under CC BY-SA 4.0 (https://creativecommons.org/licenses/by-sa/4.0/deed. **Lower Right:** Kuala Lumpur Hospital, Kuala Lumpur, Malaysia (https://commons.wikimedia.org/wiki/File:Kuala_Lumpur_Hospital.JPG) by Wikimedia user 'Chongkian'. This image is licensed under CC BY-SA 4.0 (https://creativecommons.org/licenses/by-sa/4.0/deed.en).

Dean Danaraj was a visionary. He started his medical academic career in 1946 at the King Edward College of Medicine in Singapore. He rose to become Dean of postgraduate medical education in 1960. In 1962, he was invited to become the foundation Dean, Faculty of Medicine, University Malaya. He went into action immediately to raise the faculty.

He planned the faculty building meticulously, and the departments had extra floor spaces for future expansion. The hospital was carefully designed with a modern layout of the wards and other facilities. He had an eye for detail and was a strict disciplinarian. He would pay frequent impromptu visits to the departments to see their functioning. He would often end up in conflicts with the faculty staff, and he was more feared than loved by the staff. As a professor of Medicine, he was an excellent bedside teacher, but here again, he would end up clashing with the students. He was also a good researcher and had several publications in international journals to his credit.

Teaching started, and the English language was the medium of instruction. A co-education system was followed. Most students admitted were Chinese, with the rest being Malays and Indians in almost equal numbers. The best-performing students were mostly Chinese. The students were well-behaved and respected their teachers irrespective of whether they were Malaysian or expatriates. The students responsibly interacted with their teachers. They were well-behaved in the lectures and only became uncomfortable if the teacher could not make them understand or was presenting too difficult lecture material beyond their comprehension. Most students were eager to learn and visited the teachers' offices for clarifications on a given lecture. Tutorial and practical sessions were held as small group teaching to clarify individual student learning issues. During my twelve years of stay, I did not witness any strike or demonstration by the students over any issue. The only time when the faculty and the university were closed for an extended period was during the communal disturbances of 1969. After the riots were over, the faculty reopened, and the students of all three ethnic groups mixed like before the riots without any prejudices.

External examiners from the English-speaking world were invited to the department once a year to examine the students in the final examination. They were top-ranking Physiologists, and I developed contacts with many of them. When I shifted to Kuwait Medical Faculty, I used to invite them there. The faculty developed contacts with the Royal Australasian College of Surgeons to hold their Part 1 course and examination for the Malaysian students in our faculty. I was appointed by the Royal College as one of the examiners for the Part 1 course.

The academic staff established their research laboratories, and in due course, publications started appearing in International journals. The University of Malaya had meagre resources for research funding in those days. I had enough yearly research funding from the university to pay for the consumable items. I was also getting research funding from the Welcome Trust of London. The university will give research travel support once every three years. I used to get financial support from local industry sources to supplement my research travel. The research publications from the faculty in international journals picked up both in quality and quantity, and the University of Malaya Faculty of Medicine was recognized by its peers as the leading medical school in the Southeast Asian region.

Figure 4.4: The frontal facade of the Kuala Lumpur railway station (Rawang-Seremban/Sentul-Port Klang line), Kuala Lumpur, Malaysia. (https://commons.wikimedia.org/wiki/File:Kuala_Lumpur_railway_station_(Rawang-Seremban_%26_Sentul-Port_Klang_Line)_(frontal_facade),_Kuala_Lumpur.jpg) by Wikimedia user 'Two hundred per cent'. This image is licensed under CC BY-SA 2.5 (https://creativecommons.org/licenses/by-sa/2.5/deed.en). The "Neo Moorish/Mughal/Indo-Saracenic/Neo-Saracenic" style of Kuala Lumpur Railway Station was completed in 1917 during British colonial rule.

After getting married, my wife and I arrived in Kuala Lumpur on November 1, 1968, to join the Department of Physiology, Faculty of Medicine. Prof. Gordon Ring, Chairman of the department, received us at the airport. The university arranged for us to stay at the iconic Majestic Hotel facing the colonial-style Moorish building of the Kuala Lumpur railway station. Majestic, a heritage hotel, was built in 1932 and became one of the great hotels of Kuala Lumpur in its time. The hotel became the place of glamorous private receptions, government receptions, and prominent residences for international visitors. We spent an enjoyable one week in this hotel at the university's expense before we were relocated to a fully furnished flat in the university staff residential area. The flat had a large balcony facing a lush green valley. We settled down there, and I joined the Department of Physiology.

Professor Gordon Ring, the department's chairman, was a retired senior physiologist from Florida, USA. The China Medical Board appointed him for three years. The other appointee was Associate Professor Arthur Brown from Seattle, USA. With a physics background, Prof. Brown was innovative in designing research gadgets. We developed a good rapport, and years later, when I shifted to Kuwait, I invited him to my department as a visiting professor and, later, for a continuous stay of three years. Prof Brown was an excellent and innovative teacher and had been rated as the best teacher in physiology by the students wherever he taught, including Kuala Lumpur and Kuwait. Other departments' academic staff included one Sri Lankan Malaysian, two Malaysian Chinese, and one Malaysian Indian. The laboratory staff was a mix of Chinese and Indian technicians.

The only Malay in the department was a bottom-rung attendant, Jadi. Jadi was a polite, humble, and respectful young man interested in cultivating and hosting foreigners in his modest house. I was just a few months into the department when, around Muslim Eid time, he invited Arthur Brown and me for lunch in his shanty house in one of the Kampongs of the city. We, accompanied by our wives, visited his house for lunch. He laid a big table outside his hut, and his wife, who cooked the food, arranged various homemade Malay dishes. The dishes included nasi lemak, beef rending, and meat and vegetable curries. It was very delicious Malay food, and we enjoyed it. It was the first Malay food I had tasted, and that too in the shanty house of the son of the soil (Bumiputra). In the coming years, the government built multistory housing blocks and most Kampong dwellers were relocated to one or two-bedroom apartments. Jadi was also relocated. Once he settled down, he invited us for lunch to show us his new apartment with pride.

Chapter 5

SOCIAL AND CULTURAL LIFE

The social life of all the ethnic Asian communities of Malaysia revolved around their extended families. The family was the central point of social hierarchies, and their social status determined the family interaction. The head of the family is respected and guides the family's destiny. The family supports the needy members, provides them with financial support, and protects them from their adversaries. Relationships between the families are also developed, and status determines the level of engagement. Family structure is highly evolved among the Indian communities. Because of this, it was common to see married sons staying with their parents despite the inherent conflicts it creates within the family.

Malaysians usually develop social family circles among friends for entertainment and amusement. They meet periodically in their houses over dinner and drinks. Cooperation and loyalty are valued in Malaysian families. Family social circles are also common among Malaysian Indians, particularly in the Sikh community.

Multicultural Malaysian society is enriched through the age-old traditions of its diverse population. The traditional festivities of each community amuse the population, though the festivities do not spill over and get a part of other communities. Each community has its brand of festivities that captivate the others.

The major Malay festivities occur during the Muslim holidays: Hari Raya Puasa (Holiday of Fasting) and Eid al Fitr, celebrated at the end of the fasting month. The end of the pilgrimage to Mecca marks the celebration of Hari Raya Haji or Eid al-Adha. During the Eid holidays, Malay greet the family and each other and distribute sweets and food. During these holidays, Malays visit mosques and offer prayers. Non-Malays also welcome Malays on such occasions.

Figure 5.1. Múa lân trong lễ hội làng Triều Khúc (Lion Dance in Trieu Khuc Village Festival) (https://web.archive.org/web/20161023111016/http://www.panoramio.com/photo/6953551) by Vũ Hùng. This image is licensed under CC BY-SA 3.0 (https://creativecommons.org/licenses/by-sa/3.0).

Figure 5.2. Dai Loong (Big Dragon) (https://www.flickr.com/photos/avlxyz/2254962420/) by Flickr user 'Alpha'. This image is licensed under CC BY-SA 2.0 (https://creativecommons.org/licenses/by-sa/2.0/deed.en). Big Dragon Dance.

The major festival of Malaysian Chinese is the Chinese New Year. The celebrations are usually family- and community-based—some Orthodox Chinese visit religious temples, but most Chinese celebrate it socially. The troupes of Lion and Dragon dancers perform in the streets of Chinese-dominated cities in Malaysia.

Figure 5.3. Diwali Festival (celebrated by Hindus all over the world). Shown here is the arrangement of Diyas (oil lamps) on Diwali Night (https://www. flickr.com/photos/69871685@N05/6916052573/sizes/o/in/photostream/) by Ashish Kanitkar. This image is licensed under CC BY-SA 2.0 (https:// creativecommons.org/licenses/by-sa/2.0/).

Figure 5.4. House with Lights during the Diwali Festival (https://commons. wikimedia.org/wiki/File:DiwaliKarnal.JPG) by Arne Hückelheim. This image is licensed under CC BY-SA 3.0 (https://creativecommons.org/ licenses/by-sa/3.0/).

The major festival of Malaysian Indians(Hindus and Sikhs) is Deepavali, the festival of Lights. Tamils also celeberate Thaipusam.On the night of Deepavali, Indians, including Sikhs, decorate the front of their houses with lights. Cultural dances are also performed to celebrate the event.

Figure 5.5. Surajkund Crafts Mela (https://www.flickr.com/photos/kkoshy/5426724270/) by Flickr user 'Koshy Koshy.' This image is licensed under CC BY 2.0 (https://creativecommons.org/licenses/by/2.0/deed.en#).

Figure 5.6. Thaipusam, Penang (https://commons.wikimedia.org/wiki/File:Penang_thaipusam_Silver_chariot.jpg) by Wikimedia user 'Dassmahen.' This image is licensed under CC BY-SA 4.0. (https://creativecommons.org/licenses/by-sa/4.0/deed.en).

Figure 5.7. A Day of Devotion – Thaipusam in Singapore (https://www.flickr.com/photos/adforce1/4316108409/) by William Cho. This image is licensed under CC BY SA 2.0 (https://creativecommons.org/licenses/by-sa/2.0/deed.en). Ritual Piercing during Thaipusam. The woman is carrying a Kavadi.

Thaipusam is an important festival of South Indian Tamils. In Kuala Lumpur, it is celebrated at the Batu Caves temple. This festival has dance performances and rituals piercing the body.

Figure 5.8. Bhangra Dancers in Punjab, India (https://commons.wikimedia.org/wiki/File:Bhangra-dance.jpg) by Wikimedia user 'Jaipuneetsingh.' This image is licensed under CC BY-SA 4.0 (https://creativecommons.org/licenses/by-sa/4.0/deed.en).

The Sikh community in Malaysia also celebrated their important ethnic festivals. We used to participate in them. One of the festivals celebrated is the Harvest Festival or Baisakhi in April every year. The celebrations centre around a vigorous dance by a troupe of dancers called Bhangra Dance. It is the traditional dance performed during this festival.

All three communities celebrated their religious festivals with enthusiasm. People would visit their holy places to offer prayers and celebrations at home. Christians in the country also celebrate their religious festivals with equal enthusiasm. Official holidays are declared for Muslim religious festivals, including extended holidays for Eid celebrations. Holidays were also announced for Diwali, Chinese New Year, Christmas, and New Year on the Gregorian calendar. On these holidays, it was customary to hold an "open house" where guests from other communities were treated to various ethnic delicacies. A holiday for all the ethnic and religious communities of the country is Hari Kebangsaan (National Day), which celebrates Malaysia's independence on August 31st of every year.

While in Malaysia, we developed friendships with several families, mainly from the Sikh community. Sikhs from Punjab carry their tradition of legendary hospitality to foreign lands. Lavish food cooked in the tradition of the Punjab villages was always served. The food was chased with whiskey, the preferred drink of the Punjabis. White Label scotch whiskey was served in the same way as the best brandy was served in the Chinese dinner parties. We also used to travel to other cities in Malaysia to socialize with our friends there, as well as to Singapore and Bangkok.

In addition to social and religious events, important family life events are also celebrated. Birthdays of children and sometimes adults were very elaborately celebrated. We used to mark the birthdays of our school-going daughters when many families and their children were invited to a gala dinner. Among the Malay community, the circumcision of young boys was a very special occasion and celebrated by a feast known in Malay as *Kenduri*. Marriages in the communities were another special occasion for celebration. Various communities celebrate marriages according to their ethnic traditions, with a lot of singing and dancing and gorgeous food and drinks. Usually, these celebrations in the cities were held in hotels.

The history and culture of Malaysia are preserved in various museums in its cities. In Kuala Lumpur, the largest museum, Museum Negara or National Museum, displays Malaysia's ancient history and diverse archaeological and ethnographic collections. It was built in 1963. The collections document Malaysia's social, cultural, architectural, artistic, and economic history. I visited the museum during my tenure of duty in Kuala Lumpur.

Figure 5.9. Muzium Negara (National Museum), Kuala Lumpur (https://commons.wikimedia.org/wiki/File:Muzium_Negara_Malaysia_KL_(2022-05).jpg) by Wikimedia user 'Chainwit.'. This image is licensed under CC BY-SA 4.0 (https://creativecommons.org/licenses/by-sa/4.0/deed.en).

Other cities of Peninsular Malaya have museums preserving their cultural and social history. The Perak Museum in Taiping is the oldest in Peninsular Malaysia and displays collections of natural history and artistic objects. Penang Museum has an art gallery preserving the history of colonial rule and immigrants to the island.

In the late sixties of the last century, there were few institutions to document and preserve Malaysian social and cultural traditions. I visited a national museum, an art gallery, and some theatres for performing arts. However, in subsequent years, other museums, theatres, galleries, and art museums were added. *The National Art Gallery* exhibits paintings by Malaysian artists and exhibitions by artists from around the world. Islamic Cultural Museum traces the advent of Islam from the 7th century onwards. Many other topical museums have also come up. One of the most noted is the *Istana Budaya or Palace of Culture*. It is the grand theatre of Kuala Lumpur, where plays, musicals, and dances are performed by Malaysian artists and by artists from around the world. The Istana Budaya was opened in 1999. It is located next to the National Art Gallery in Kuala Lumpur.

Figure 5.10. National Museum, Kuala Lumpur. **Upper Left**: Avalokiteshvara statue found at Anglo Oriental, Bidor, Perak (https://commons. wikimedia.org/wiki/File:Muzium_Negara_KL67.JPG) by Wikimedia user 'Gryffindor.' This image is licensed under CC BY 3.0 (https:// creativecommons.org/licenses/by/3.0/). **Upper Right:** The Main Hall of the National MuseuminKualaLumpur(https://commons.wikimedia.org/ wiki/File:National_Museum_KL_2008_interior_pano.jpg) by Wikimedia user 'Gryffindor'. This image is in the public domain. **Lower Left**: Carts at the National Museum in KualaLumpur(https://commons.wikimedia. org/wiki/File:National_Museum_KL_2008_157_pano.jpg) by Wikimedia user 'Gryffindor.' This image is in the public domain. **Lower Right:** Istana Satu (https://commons.wikimedia.org/wiki/File:National_Museum_KL_ 2008_Istana_pano.jpg) by Wikimedia user 'Gryffindor.' This image is in the public domain. *'Upper Left*: A statue was found at the tin mine Bidor, Perak, in 1936, and it is an 8th- 9th-century bronze statue. *Upper Right:* View of the main hall of the museum. *Lower Left*: Historic carts in the National Museum. On the left is the Johar Horse Cart (Kreta Kudur Johar). Used by the Chinese community for transportation,c. 1900. It was later commercialized as public transport. On the right is the Malacca Bullock Cart (Kreta Lembu Malacca). A heritage cart and symbol of Malacca was introduced in the Malacca Sultanate around the 15th century by Indian traders. *Lower Right:* Istana Satu was erected by the Sultan of Terengganu in 1884. The building has traditional Malay architecture. The building was re-erected in the compound of the National Museum in 1974.'

Figure 5.11. **Left:** National Art Gallery of Malaysia (https://commons. wikimedia.org/wiki/File:Balai_Seni_Negara.jpg) by Wikimedia user 'Wee Hong'. This image is licensed under CC BY-SA 4.0 (https://creativecommons. org/licenses/by-sa/4.0/deed.en) **Right:** Istana Budaya from Lake View (https://commons.wikimedia.org/wiki/File:Istana_Budaya_from_lake_ view.jpg) by Wikimedia user 'Whjayg.' This image is licensed under CC BY-SA 4.0 (https://creativecommons.org/licenses/by-sa/4.0/deed.en).

The port city of Malacca became the region's economic and cultural hub from the 13th to 17th centuries CE. The port was established around 1400 by Sumatran exiles. The Indianised King successfully became a tributary state of China. Trade was needed to raise money for the tribute. The overseas trade was in the hands of Middle Eastern Islamic merchants, and later, in the 15th century, it was also done by Indian Islamic merchants. These merchants pressured the king to convert to Islam to trade with them. The Hindu king of Malacca converted to Islam and became a Sultan. In due course, Malacca became the centre of Islam, from where Islam spread to other parts of Southeast Asia. Muslim merchants were attracted to Malacca. Malacca became the regional trading hub and became rich. In the 15th century, at its height, the free port of Malacca hosted 15,000 merchants from different nationalities, including Chinese, Arabs, Persians, and Indians. The Malaccan experience spread to the whole of peninsular Malaya, and the Islamatized people started calling themselves Malays and the term was applied to people who professed Islam. During this period, Malay culture and economy flourished.

Chapter 6

TOURISTIC CITIES OF PENINSULA

Peninsular Malaya in the north shares a land border with Thailand. On the southern tip, across the straits of Johar, it shares a maritime border with Singapore.In between lies the land mass of the Peninsula, with its west coast washed by the Indian Ocean and the east coast by the South China Sea. A central mountainous range with tertiary jungles divides the Peninsula. Major cities and towns are located on the flatlands of the west coast and north of the Peninsula. The islands of Penang and Pulau Langkawi are situated off the west coast.

The *Island of Penang* is separated from the mainland by the Penang Straits. Two major bridges connect Penang Island with the mainland.

Figure 6.1. Butterworth and Penang Scenery (https://www.flickr.com/photos/marufish/314093535400) by Flickr user 'Marufish.' This image is licensed under CC BY-SA 2.0 (https://creativecommons.org/licenses/by-sa/2.0/). The Penang Bridge.

Figure 6.2. Old Town of Georgetown, Penang. (https://commons.wikimedia.org/wiki/File:Old_town_of_Georgetown..JPG) by Wikimedia user 'Milei. Vencel'. This image is licensed under CC BY-SA 3.0 (https://creativecommons.org/licenses/by-sa/3.0/). The Historic City Centre of Georgetown.Now a World Heritage Site by UNESCO.

Figure 6.3. **Left:** Weld Quay in the Port of Penang, Georgetown (https://commons.wikimedia.org/wiki/File:KITLV_-_80020_-_Kleingrothe,_C.J._-_Medan_-_Quay_in_Penang_-_circa_1910.tif) by Kleingrothe, Carl Josef, sourced from Royal Netherlands Institute of Southeast Asian and Caribbean Studies and Leiden University Library/ Wikimedia Commons. This image is in the public domain. **Right:** Penang Malaysia Sunrise at Tanjong Bungah Mosque (https://www.flickr.com/ photos/shebalso/4461552447/) by Flickr user 'John.' This image is licensed under CC BY-SA 2.0. (https://creativecommons.org/licenses/by-sa/2.0/). Floating Mosque of Tanjung Bungah, Penang.

The history of Penang was shaped by British colonialism in the 18th century CE. The British East India Company acquired the island from the Sultan of Kedah in 1786 for trading purposes. British explorer Francis Light, on Company pay, founded the British colony of Penang with the newly developed capital, George Town. King George III (1760-1801) ruled the British Empire, and the capital city of Penang was named after him. This name, George Town, is still enduring. It was developed into a free port. By the end of the 19th century CE, George Town had become prosperous and a major port for re-export in Southeast Asia.

The population of George Town swelled with a major influx of Chinese and others, and trade flourished. The

British colonial government started building several administrative buildings. The High Court of Penang was established in 1801, the first judiciary building in Malaya. Many other iconic buildings were constructed, and some with old harbours are well preserved.

Penang is a popular tourist destination both for regional and international tourists. One can explore Penang's colonial history by visiting various well-preserved European architectural style buildings of the 19th century CE. The three major ethnic communities inhabiting Penang have their religious worship places. There are several mosques for the Malays, but the most prominent is the Floating Mosque of Tanjong Bungah. Penang is full of temples of various denominations. Several Chinese temples are devoted to Buddhism, Taoism, and Confucianism, and one snake temple contains poisonous snakes. There is also an elegant Siamese (Thai) Buddhist temple. Prominent Tamil Hindu temples of exquisite South Indian designs and stone and marble carved deities are also present.

During our twelve-year stay in Malaysia, my family and I visited Penang several times. It was one of the preferred holiday destinations. George Town was a small town where most hotels were located and owned by Chinese, though the hotels had mixed ethnic staff. There were small beachside hotels also. The iconic town centre, now a world heritage site, was well preserved and looked as if it had not changed since it was built in the 18th century

CE. There were Chinese-style shophouses with red-tiled roofs. We located two colonial-era Chinese and Indian

Figure 6.4. **Upper Left:**Penang, Malaysia: Wat Chaiya Mangkalaram Temple,(https://commons.wikimedia.org/wiki/File:Penang_Malaysia_Wat-Chaiya-Mangkalaram-Temple-01.jpg), photo by CEphoto, Uwe Aranas. This image is licensed under CC BY-SA 3.0 (https://creativecommons.org/licenses/by-sa/3.0/deed.en). **Upper Right:** Snake Temple (https://commons.wikimedia.org/wiki/File:Snake_Temple,_Penang.jpg) by Flickr user 'Khalzuri Yazid'. This image is licensed under CC BY-SA 2.0 (https://creativecommons.org/licenses/by-sa/2.0/). **Lower Left:** Kek Lok Si Temple, Georgetown, Penang (https://commons.wikimedia.org/wiki/File:Kek_Lok_Si_1.jpg), Photo/Map: Arne Müseler / arne-mueseler.com / CC-BY-SA-3.0 / https://creativecommons.org/licenses/by-sa/3.0/de/deed.de. (Kek Lok Si Tempel, Georgetown, Penang (https://commons.wikimedia.org/wiki/File:Kek_Lok_Si_1.jpg) by Arne Müseler (arne-mueseler.com). This image is licensed under CC BY-SA 3.0 (https://creativecommons.org/licenses/by-sa/3.0/de/deed.de). **Lower Right:** A Hindu Temple Beside the Bird Park (https://www.flickr.com/photos/shankaronline/12340299965/) by Flickr user 'Shankar S.' This image is licensed under CC BY 2.0 (https://creativecommons.org/licenses/by/2.0/deed.en#).

'Temples of Penang. *Upper Left*: Wat Chayamankalaram Siamese temple, constructed in 1845 in colonial Penang on the land gifted by Queen Victoria. *Upper Right*: Chinese Snake Temple in Byan Lepas, Penang. The devotees perform snake dance in the temple during the night. Live viper snakes are kept inside the temple, ostensibly for worship. *Lower Left*: Kek Lok Si Temple, one of the largest Chinese temples in Penang. *Lower Right*: Karumariamman Temple is a Tamil Indian Temple in Penang. The architecture reflects the ancient South Indian Hindu Temple design.'

restaurants serving authentic Chinese and Indian food, which we have always visited when in the town. There were no high-rise buildings. It was a perfect balance between the small town, beaches, and the environment, giving us feelings of harmony and serenity. With my family, I would drive my Volkswagen car from Kuala Lumpur to Butterworth, the mainland ferry terminal, park my car, and catch a ferry to the island. There were no sea bridges in those days. We used to visit all the tourist places on the island, including colonial buildings and temples, and hop on the funicular railway up Penang Hill, the tallest point on the island. Beautiful views of the island from the hill and the sea waters lashing the beaches were enchanting. We used to enjoy Chinese food from the hilltop restaurant in this lovely ambience.

The Penang beaches were the most beautiful deep-water beaches with crystal-clear water. In the seventies and last century, the beaches were unspoiled, unlike today's beaches, with a modest number of local and foreign tourists, primarily European, visiting Penang.

The modern Penang Island is another story. The island is highly commercialized, with high-rise buildings dotted all over, and the city area of George Town is now a concrete jungle. When Francis Light of the East India Company landed on the island in 1786, it was covered with a dense jungle. He cleared the jungle to establish a hamlet in George Town. In subsequent years, the Chinese built typical shophouses and created the city centre, fortunately preserved and listed as a World Heritage Site by UNESCO. Today, George Town is a small metropolis full of high-rise buildings and hectic commercial activity. It was a significant transformation from a small, sleepy town of yesteryears to a commercialized city, betraying its holiday culture.

Penang is known for its "unique architecture and cultural townscape," which the British colonial rulers contributed and augmented by the immigrant communities of Chinese and Indians. The old city centre area has classic restaurants catering to the traditional food of Chinese, Indian, and Malay communities. The city is also sometimes termed the gastronomic capital of Malaya.

Figure 6.5. **Left:** Khoo Kongsi (https://commons.wikimedia.org/wiki/File:Khoo_Kongsi_(cropped_to_4_to_3_format).jpg) by Supanut Arunoprayote. This image is licensed under CC BY 4.0 (https://creativecommons.org/licenses/by/4.0/deed.en). **Right:** Penang City Hall (https://commons.wikimedia.org/wiki/File:Penang_City_Hall_(cropped).jpg) by Supanut Arunoprayote. This image is licensed under CC BY-SA 4.0 (https://creativecommons.org/licenses/by-sa/4.0/deed.en). Well-preserved British Colonial Building.

A highly Ornamental Chinese Clan House (Khoo Kongsi) of ancient design was erected in Penang by a prominent wealthy Chinese (towkay) from the olden days.

Langkawi, or The Jewel of Kedah, is now a duty-free island and archipelago situated off the coast of the northwestern Malay Peninsula and a few kilometres south of the Thai border. The island has been developed as a major tourist resort with an international airport. During my stay in Malaysia in the seventies, there was little development of the island, and it remained a backwater till 1986, when the then Prime Minister of Malaysia, who hailed from the state of Kedah, started a significant development of the island and refurbished the city centre areas of Kuah, the capital of the island. The island rapidly grew, and by 2012, it started receiving three million tourists a year.

However, recently, the island's popularity has been dented by a declining number of tourists visiting the island.

Figure 6.6. **Left:** The skyline of downtown George Town as seen from the Penang Straits in December 2023 (https://commons.wikimedia.org/wiki/File:Panorama_of_George_Town_from_the_air,_Dec_2023.jpg) by Wikimedia user 'HundenvonPenang'. This image is licensed under CC BY-SA 4.0 (https://creativecommons.org/licenses/by-sa/4.0/deed.en). **Right:** A Funicular Tram Ascending Penang Hill in June 2023 (https://commons.wikimedia.org/wiki/File:Penang_Hill_funicular_railway.jpg) by Wikimedia user 'HundenvonPenang'. This image is licensed under CC BY-SA 4.0 (https://creativecommons.org/licenses/by-sa/4.0/deed.en). *Left:* The city centre of George Town in 2023, with the view of Penang Hill in the background. The present-day city centre is full of concrete low and high-rise buildings, masking the olden days' pristine beauty. *Right:* Penang Hill was approached by the present-day funicular trains in 2023. Old models of these trains operated much earlier. In the early seventies, we had a ride on them.'

During my tenure in the country, in the mid-seventies, I used to load my Volkswagen with my family and drive north to Kuala Perlis, the northernmost part of the Peninsula, touching the Thai border. The car was left in Kuala Perlis, and we took a boat ride to the island. We stayed in a beach-facing hotel. The beaches of Langkawi, its sands, and the natural ambience of the surrounding small islands offered unmatched beauty and serenity. We would lay on the white sands, dip in the clear waters of the beach, sit under the shade of palm trees, sip a chilled beer, and visualize the Paradise of nature on earth.

There was not much tourist traffic when I visited Langkawi. Foreign tourists, mostly Germans, would take a boat ride from the beaches of neighbouring Thailand and spend time on the beaches of Langkawi. The small town of Kuah had the usual Chinese shophouses and restaurants serving Chinese, Indian, and Malay cuisine.

Figure 6.7. **Left:** Penang Bridge (https://www.flickr.com/photos/s-a-m/267766337/) by Flickr user 'Samantha.' This image is licensed under CC BY 2.0 (https://creativecommons.org/licenses/by/2.0/deed.en#). **Right:** Langkawi, Maha Tower (https://commons.wikimedia.org/wiki/File:Langkawi_20230317.jpg) by Wikimedia user 'RA1828'. This image is licensed under CC BY-SA 4.0 (https://creativecommons.org/licenses/by-sa/4.0/deed.en).

Figure 6.8. **Left:** Telaga Tujoh Waterfalls,(https://commons.wikimedia. org/wiki/File:Telaga_tujuh_waterfalls.jpg) by Wikimedia user 'Sabrinakhanpoly'. This image is licensed under CC BY-SA 4.0 (https:// creativecommons.org/licenses/by-sa/4.0/deed.en). **Right:** Structure in CHOGM Park, KuahTown,Langkawi(https://commons.wikimedia.org/ wiki/File:CHOGM_park_in_Langkawi.jpg) by Wikimedia user 'Hzh.' This image is licensed under CC BY-SA 4.0 (https://creativecommons.org/ licenses/by-sa/4.0/deed.en).

There was nothing much to see except the beauty of the beaches and several small surrounding islands visible only when the tide was low. After the significant developments of the islands in recent years, several tourist attractions have been created: the mascot of Langkawi Island, Langkawi Sky Bridge, cable car, underwater world Langkawi, Aquabeat Water Theme Park, CHOGM Park, and Oriental Village. Almost all of these attractions appeared after the major development of the island in 1986.

Cameron Highlands, developed in the 1930s, is a tableland and one of the oldest hill resorts in Malaysia. It was named after Willian Cameron, a colonial explorer and geologist. He recommended the tableland, located in the eastern state of Pahang, be developed as a hill resort because of its pleasant cool climate and exotic views of the central mountainous terrain of the Peninsula. A road was extended from Tapah town, in Perak state, to the highlands in 1931; settlements alongside the road soon appeared, and the hill resort was developed. The resort is located 200 kilometres from Kuala Lumpur. The township of Brinchang in the flatlands served as the main resort town with a city centre, hotels, and other tourist facilities.

Figure 6.9. **Left:** The Township of Brinchang, Cameron Highlands, Pahang, West Malaysia (https://commons.wikimedia.org/wiki/File:TIME_TUNNEL_museum11a.jpg) by See Kok Shan. This image is licensed under CC BY-SA 3.0 (https://creativecommons.org/licenses/by-sa/3.0/). **Right:** View of Fields and Fields of Tea (https://www.flickr.com/photos/wills/119867512/) by Flickr user 'Will Ellis. This image is licensed under CC BY 2.0 (https://creativecommons.org/licenses/by/2.0/deed.en#).

Until 1965, Cameron Highlands was the only major hill station in Malaysia, becoming popular with local and British tourists. With the development of Genting Highlands resort, many tourists preferred this resort because of its proximity to Kuala Lumpur. Close to one million tourists visited Camron Highlands in 2022.

Genting Highlands was established in the mountains of the central Peninsula in the state of Pahang in 1965 by a Malaysian entrepreneur, Lim Goh Tong. The resort is 58 Km from Kuala Lumpur and can be reached by a good road. As it has become lately, Resorts World Genting boasts theme parks and casinos where gambling is permitted. Recent developments of the resort include several skyscrapers and luxury hotels. Because of its proximity to Kuala Lumpur and legal gambling, the resort has flourished rapidly and draws tourists from Malaysia, Singapore, and other countries.

I visited the resort in the mid-1970s, and it was developing fast. The Genting town was bustling with tourists, primarily Chinese. New hotels were opening up, and Chinese food restaurants offered excellent food. Located at 1880 meters, it provided a refreshing, cool climate, a stark contrast to the hot, humid climate of Kuala Lumpur. Developments of the resort in recent years include two cable cars to provide access to the resort, Genting Grand indoor theme park, Genting outdoor theme park, Arena of Stars, and First World Plaza. These attractions were built between 1992 and 2001. Several hotels opened up to accommodate the ever-increasing number of tourists. In addition to the entertainment activities, the resort offers breathtaking views of the highlands. The resort's popularity grew exponentially; in 2022, it received 22.2 million tourists, about 77% of the pre-epidemic level. With the opening up of Genting, the lure for Cameron

Highlands diminished, and in 2022, only one million tourists visited it.

Figure 6.10. **Upper Left:** The Main Entrance for Genting Skyworlds Theme Park (https://commons.wikimedia.org/wiki/File:Genting_Skyworld_Theme_Park%27s_Main_Entrance.jpg) by Wikimedia user 'Dulcetia.' This image is licensed under CC BY-SA 4.0 (https://creativecommons.org/licenses/by-sa/4.0/deed.en). **Upper Right:** Resorts World Genting (https://www.flickr.com/photos/chleong/2966453599/sizes/o/in/photostream/) by Chee Hong. This image is licensed under CC BY 2.0 (https://creativecommons.org/licenses/by/2.0/deed.en#). **Lower Left:** Genting Grand Hotel, Genting Highlands, Bentong, Pahang, Malaysia (https://commons.wikimedia.org/wiki/File:Genting_Grand_Hotel.jpg) by Wikimedia user 'Chongkian'. This image is licensed under CC BY-SA 4.0 (https://creativecommons.org/licenses/by-sa/4.0/deed.en. **Lower Right**: Genting Highlands, Malaysia: Hall and Pagoda of the Chin Swee Caves Temple (https://commons.wikimedia.org/wiki/File:Genting-Highlands_Malaysia_Chin-Swee-Caves-Temple-02.jpg), photo by CEphoto, Uwe Aranas. This image is licensed under CC BY-SA 3.0 (https://creativecommons.org/licenses/by-sa/3.0/deed.en).

Malacca is located in the southern region of the Malay Peninsula, facing the Straits of Malacca. Malacca is a historic town that preserves the region's five centuries of history. Malacca was a small fishing village before Raja Parameswara, a Hindu Malay chief, arrived in 1404 after being expelled from Singapore by the invading Javanese. He developed Malacca into a significant regional trading seaport and promoted trade relations with Chinese, Arab Muslims, and Indian Muslim traders. The Muslim traders influenced him to accept Islam, and he changed his name to Iskander Shah, and Islam became the state religion of Malaya. To fend off the nagging attacks from neighbouring Siam, Malacca became a protectorate and a tributary state of China.

European colonizers arrived in Malacca in the early 16th century CE. They were headed by the Portuguese, who, in 1511, sailed from their colony of Goa in India. They occupied Malacca and established their control till the arrival of the Dutch in the seventeenth century. The Portuguese built a fort and the first church in Southeast Asia; their ruins can still be seen. The Duch defeated the Portuguese and occupied Malacca from 1641 to 1796.

The Dutch built the landmark building in the heart of Malacca, the Stadthuys or City Hall, in 1650. The building is still there in good condition. This historical, remaining Dutch building in Southeast Asia is now a History and Ethnography Museum.

Figure 6.11. **Upper Left**: The only surviving remains of the Porta de Santiago in the Portuguese Fort (https://commons.wikimedia.org/wiki/File:A_Famosa_Malacca.JPG) by Wikimedia user 'T0lk'. This image is dedicated to the public domain. **Upper Right:** St Paul Church, Malacca (https://commons.wikimedia.org/wiki/File:St_Paul_Church_Malacca_7.jpg) by Wikimedia user 'Gryffindor.' This image is licensed under CC BY-SA 3.0 (https://creativecommons.org/licenses/by-sa/3.0/). **Lower Left**: Bastion Middleburg, Malacca Town, Malacca, Malaysia (https://commons.wikimedia.org/wiki/File:Bastion_Middleburg.JPG) by Wikimedia user 'Chongkian.' This image is licensed under CC BY-SA 4.0 (https://creativecommons.org/licenses/by-sa/4.0/deed.en) **Lower Right:** The Replica of Malacca Sultanate Palace is a Historical Museum (https://commons.wikimedia.org/wiki/File:Malacca_Sultanate_Palace.JPG) by Wikimedia user 'Adiput.' This image is dedicated to the public domain. *'Upper Right*: Ruins of St Paul's Church in Malacca built in 1521. *Lower Left*: The bastion Middleburgh was constructed in Malacca by the Dutch in 1660. '

The Dutch handed over Malacca to the British in the 19th century CE during the British occupation of the

Islands of Penang and Singapore. While the islands were well developed by the British colonizers, the development of Malacca was neglected. Instead, the British started developing Kuala Lumpur as the capital of their Malayan colony. Malacca remains a historical tourist attraction with some well-preserved colonial artefacts.

Figure 6.12. The Stadhuys in Malacca (https://commons.wikimedia.org/wiki/File:Malacca_stadhuys1.jpg) by Elizabeth Lisa John. This image is licensed under CC BY 1.0 (https://creativecommons.org/licenses/by/1.0/deed.en).

Malacca's recreational facilities include amusement parks and water theme parks. The city preserves five centuries of history of the colonial powers, Portuguese, Dutch, and British.

Figure 6.13. **Upper Left:** Sultan Abu Bakar State Mosque, Johor Baru, Johor, Malaysia (https://commons.wikimedia.org/wiki/File:Sultan_Abu_Bakar_State_Mosque.jpg) by Wikimedia user 'Chongkian'. This image is licensed under CC BY-SA 4.0 (https://creativecommons.org/licenses/by-sa/4.0/deed.en **Upper Right:** Sultan Palace in Johor Baru (Malaysia) (https://commons.wikimedia.org/wiki/File:SultanPalastJB.jpg) by Wikimedia user 'AngMoKio.' This image is licensed under CC BY-SA 3.0 (https://creativecommons.org/licenses/by-sa/3.0/). **Lower Left:** Road viaducts leading from the Bangunan Sultan Iskandar checkpoint (foreground) to the Johor Baru-Singapore Causeway (https://commons.wikimedia.org/wiki/File:Causeway_12.jpg) by Wikimedia user 'Slleong.' This image is dedicated to the public domain under CC0 1.0 (https://creativecommons.org/publicdomain/zero/1.0/?ref=chooser-v1). **Lower Right:** Johar Baru Skyline from Woodland Pier.

Johar Baru is the capital of the southern state of Johar and sits on the south tip of the Peninsula on the banks of the Straits of Johar. The city is the financial centre and logistics hub of the South Peninsula. Its economic status is further enhanced by its proximity to Singapore, to which a Causeway connects it. The Causeway was built in 1923 and has improved considerably in recent years. We visited the city several times by road on our way to Singapore. In those days, the city was not well developed. Modern development started in recent years when several high-rise buildings appeared and changed the skyline of Johar Baru.

Kuala Lumpur, the capital of Malaysia, is now a bustling modern metropolis with an impressive skyline. But in the 1970s, it was a small sleeping town full of Chinese-style shophouses and a few multi-floor buildings but no skyscrapers. The intersection of Jalan Tuanku Abdul Rahaman and Jalan Mountbatten, the city's main streets, marked the city centre. Besides the city centre are colonial Moorish-style administrative buildings and the iconic Selangor club facing the Padang (green pitch). Adjoining these buildings towards the west is the Moorish-Indian building of the celebrated railway station, and facing it across the road is the colonial-era Majestic Hotel. These buildings are well preserved. The city had other hotels of different categories, but two four-star hotels stand out: Hotel Merlin and the Federal Hotel. During the colonial era, Hotel Majestic served to house the visiting dignitaries and officials, but after liberation, Hotel Merlin functioned as such. For over 100 years, the old city's central market for groceries and household supplies has existed and functioned in its original form till today. In the 1970s, it was a Chinese-dominated town with the Chinatown of Petaling Street and the recreational area of Bukit Bintang with its red-light district. The newly built city's Merdeka Stadium was an attraction. The city also had a well-appointed lake garden with a beautiful lake. The high-profile lake club and the Malaysian Parliament building were also located in the lake garden.

Figure 6.14. **Left**: Kuala Lumpur, Malaysia: Bangunan Parlimen Malaysia (Parliament) (https://commons.wikimedia.org/wiki/File:Kuala_Lumpur_Malaysia_Bangunan_Parlimen_Malaysia-01.jpg), photo by CEphoto, Uwe Aranas. This image is licensed under CC BY-SA 3.0 (https://creativecommons.org/licenses/by-sa/3.0/deed.en. **Right:** Kuala Lumpur, Malaysia: Dewan Bandaraya Kuala Lumpur (Kuala Lumpur City Hall) (https://commons.wikimedia.org/wiki/File:Kuala_Lumpur_Malaysia_Dewan-Bandaraya-Kuala-Lumpur-01.jpg), photo by CEphoto, Uwe Aranas. This image is licensed under the CCBY-SA 3.0 (https://creativecommons.org/licenses/by-sa/3.0/deed.en

The satellite town of Petaling Jaya, a few kilometres from the city centre, was developing mainly as a residential area. At the junction of the two is the Universiti Malaya, located on the hills surrounding the beautiful Pantai Valley, where I spent twelve years.

New city development started in recent years to mirror the style of Singapore. Several high-rise buildings, skyscrapers, Towers, and office blocks mushroomed quickly, changing the skyline of Kuala Lumpur. The city also boasts new recreational areas, food courts, restaurants, hotels, and supermarkets. Other cities and towns in Malaysia are developing identically. The city's transport system has improved with elevated Skypark trains and modern highways.

OLD KUALA LUMPUR

Figure 6.15. **Left**: Governmental Office at Kuala Lumpur in Selangor (https://digitalcollections.universiteitleiden.nl/view/item/783446) by G.R. Lambert & Co. (Singapore), sourced from the Royal Netherlands Institute of Southeast Asian and Caribbean Studies and Leiden University Library/ Wikimedia Commons. This image is in the public Domain **Right**: The Facade of Central Market, Kuala Lumpur, Malaysia (https://commons. wikimedia.org/wiki/File:Central_Market_6_June_2014.JPG), by Wikimedia user 'Bearsmalaysia.' This image is licensed under CC BY-SA 3.0 (https:// creativecommons.org/licenses/by-sa/3.0/deed.en)

Iconic Central Market of Kuala Lumpur. The building is still preserved, as I used to see it during

NEW KUALA LUMPUR

Figure 6.16. **Upper:** Sunset at Kuala Lumpur (https://commons.wikimedia.org/wiki/File:Sunset_at_Kuala_Lumpur.jpg) by Wikimedia user 'YongBoi'. This image is licensed under CC BY-SA 4.0 (https://creativecommons.org/licenses/by-sa/4.0/deed.en) **Middle:** Kuala Lumpur at night (https://commons.wikimedia.org/wiki/File:Kl-skyline-at-night-2022. jpg) by Wikimedia user 'Shahee Ilyas.' This image is licensed under CC BY-SA 4.0 (https://creativecommons.org/licenses/by-sa/4.0/deed.en). **Lower:** Lake Titiwangsa in Kuala Lumpur (https://commons. wikimedia.org/wiki/File:Kuala_Lumpur_-_Titiwangsa_-_Panorama_0002. JPG), by Stefan Fussan. This image is licensed under CC BY-SA 3.0 (https://creativecommons.org/licenses/by-sa/3.0/deed.en.

NEW- KUALA LUMPUR TOWERS

Figure 6.17. Towers of Kuala Lumpur. **Left:** Photo of Merdeka 118 taken from Kuala LumpurTower (https://commons.wikimedia.org/wiki/File:Merdeka_118_20230317.jpg) by Wikimedia user 'InterEdit88'. This image is licensed under CC BY-SA 4.0,(https://creativecommons.org/licenses/by-sa/4.0/deed.en). **Middle:** Photo of the Exchange 106, taken from Kuala Lumpur Tower (https://commons.wikimedia.org/wiki/File:The_Exchange_106_20230317.jpg) by Wikimedia user 'InterEdit88'. This image is licensed under CC BY-SA 4.0 (https://creativecommons.org/licenses/by-sa/4.0/deed.en) **Right:** Petronas Tower 3 (https://commons.wikimedia.org/wiki/File:KL-_Petronas_Tower_3_on_a_rainy_morning.jpg) by Wikimedia user 'Azreey.' This image is licensed under CC BY-SA 4.0 (https://creativecommons.org/licenses/by-sa/4.0/deed.en). *'Left*: Kuala Lumpur *Menara Warisan Merdeka,* KL 118.At 679 meters, this 118-stoy Tower is the second tallest building in the world after Dubai's Burj Khalifa. *Middle: Exchange 106,* at 453.6 meters and 106 floors high, this super skyscraper is the second tallest building in Kuala Lumpur. It is the centrepiece of the Tun Razak Exchange. *Right: Petronas Tower 3* is a 60-story, 267-meter-tall skyscraper in Kuala Lumpur. The building was completed in 2011.'

Chapter 7

WHITE SANDS OF PENINSULA

Malaysian beaches are excellent tourist attractions and hubs of intriguing and refreshing recreational activities. There are coastal beaches and island beaches.

The best coastal beaches are to be found on the Peninsula's west coast; however, east coast beaches are of comparable beauty but not much explored. Because of the proximity of the beaches to the major towns, the West Coast beaches are popular with locals and tourists alike.

The Malaysian island beaches are popular with foreign tourists. There are 30 major island beaches of different degrees of beauty and serenity spread across both wings of Malaysia. Almost half of these beaches are to be found in the west wing of Peninsular Malaysia. Most of these beaches offer water sports, which may include any or more of the following: swimming, sailing, jet skiing, waterskiing, windsurfing, snorkelling, parasailing, rafting, flyboard, water polo, boating, canyoning, fishing, and so on.

Malaysia contains numerous islands, the largest being the Banggi island in Sabah, East Malaysia. The largest island on the Malaysian Peninsula is Pulau Langkawi, north of the Peninsula. Langkawi is an archipelago of several islands, offering several beaches of exotic beauty. The beaches include Pasar Cenang, Tanjung Rhu, Tengah Beach, Kok Beach, Paradise 101, Datai Bay Beach, and Teluk Yu Beach (Shark Bay). Pasar Cenang is the most beautiful beach in Langkawi. We visited it.

Figure 7.1. **Upper Left:** Cenang Beach View, Langkawi Island (https://commons.wikimedia.org/wiki/File:Cenang_Beach_view,_Langkawi.jpg) by Wikimedia user 'NickLubushko'. This image is licensed under CC BY-SA 4.0 (https://creativecommons.org/licenses/by-sa/4.0/deed.e **Upper Right:** The beach @ Langkawi, Malaysia (https://www.flickr.com/photos/timparkinson/213777728) by Tim Parkinson. This image is licensed under CC BY 2.0 (https://creativecommons.org/licenses/by/2.0/deed.en#). **Lower Left:** The Datai Langkawi - Resort Overview (https://commons.wikimedia.org/wiki/File:The_Datai_Langkawi_-_Resort_Overview.jpg) by Wikimedia user 'DataiOnline'. This image is licensed under CC BY-SA 4.0 (https://creativecommons.org/licenses/by-sa/4.0/deed.en). **Lower Right:** Penang - Malesia Panorama della spiaggia di Batu Ferringhi (https://commons.wikimedia.org/wiki/File:Batu_Ferringhi_Panorama.jpg) by Wikimedia user 'YukioSanjo'. This image is licensed under CC BY-SA 3.0 (https://creativecommons.org/licenses/by-sa/3.0/

'Beaches of Langkawi Group of Islands. *Cenang Beach of Langkawi.* It is the busiest and most developed beach in Langkawi. Its views are stunning, with white sands, clear water, and green palms. Water sports are at hand. *Tanjung (Cape) Rhu (Casuarnia trees)Beach.* The beach is located in the eastern part of Langkawi. It has clear waters of the Andaman Sea, white sands, and a cool breeze. Tall Casuarina trees line its shore, hence its name. The Casuarina tree is native to Australia and is also called she-oak. *Datai Langkawi Beach Resort.* It is a luxurious beach resort nestled in the heart of the forest. A romantic, serene retreat from the hustle and bustle of city life. It allows guests to connect with the paradise of nature in a tranquil ambience.'

Penang Island has ten of the best beaches where you can relax and enjoy the beauty of nature. The beaches include Batu Ferringhi Beach, Pulau Jerejak Beach, Tanjung Bungah Beach, Tanjung Bahang Beach, Monkey Beach, Pantai Kerachut Beach, Gertak Sanggul Beach, Pasir Panjang Beach, Teluk Kampi Beach and Moonlight Bay. Most Penang beaches have water sports facilities. Almost all the beaches are located in the northern part of the island and accessible within a 30-minute drive from the city centre.

Figure 7.2. **Left:** Bahasa Melayu: Matahari terbenam di Pulau Pangkor (The Sun Sets on Pangkor Island) (https://commons.wikimedia.org/wiki/File:Matahari_terbenam_di_Pulau_Pangkor_3.JPG) by Wikimedia user 'Izhamwong' (Ma Hzi Wong). This image is dedicated to the public domain under CC0 1.0 (https://creativecommons.org/publicdomain/zero/1.0/?ref=chooser-v1). **Right:** Lexis Hibiscus Port Dickson in Port Dickson near Kuala Lumpur International Airport, Malaysia (https://commons.wikimedia.org/wiki/File:Lexis_Hibiscus_Port_Dickson.jpg) by Anthony Ivanoff. This image is dedicated to the public domain under CC0 1.0 (https://creativecommons.org/publicdomain/zero/1.0/?ref=chooser-v1). 'Sunset at Pangkor Island viewed from the beach. *Right*: Lexis Hibiscus, Hotels and Resorts, Port Dickson. The resort, located near Kuala Lumpur International Airport, offers 'Over Water' Luxury villas and tower rooms constructed in the shape of a Hibiscus flower, the national flower of Malaysia.' It is a newer development; during my stay in the 1970s, no such luxury existed, and the beach was in its natural ambience, unspoiled by such glorious buildings.

The main and most beautiful beach of Penang Island is Batu Ferringhi Beach, which has breathtaking views. Batu Ferringhi is a suburb of George Town. The beach is located northwest of the city centre of Penang. We used to visit this beach whenever we were in Penang. The other equally attractive beach is Tangong Bungah Beach. Tanjung Bungah is a suburb of Penang about 6.5 Km from the city centre. It is a well-known beach destination with several hotels and resorts lining the beaches and high–rise residential buildings.

The beaches of the Peninsula's west coast, further south of the island of Penang, include the scenic island beaches of Pulau Pangkor. Near Kuala Lumpur is the beach of Port Dickson, which is popular with city people and foreign visitors. Malacca has on-shore and island beaches that offer well-maintained facilities. The city people visit these beaches to escape from the busy streets of Malacca. Johar Baru boasts several coastal beaches and resorts. Beaches around Johar include Pantai Air Papan Mersing, Antai Manis Tnjung Sedill, and Desaru Beach. Beaches in Johar Baru are Danga Bay and Forest City. Johar Beach Resorts include Sea Horizon Resort, The Westin Desaru, Anantara Desaru, and Sand and Sandals Desaru.

Because of their proximity to Kuala Lumpur, we frequently visited Port Dickson and Pangkor Island beaches during weekends and local holidays.

Port Dickson is an hour's drive from Kuala Lumpur, whereas Pangkor Island is three hours. In Port Dickson, we stayed at the Malaysian Railways guest house perched high on the hill, commanding breathtaking views of the Andaman Sea. The guest house was booked through our family friend, the deputy general manager of Malaysian Railways. He also gave me refuge in his Kenny Hill Bungalow during the ethnic riots of May 13, 1969, in Kuala Lumpur. The guest house had a private beach, approached by a flight of stairs down the hill. There was a Chinese caretaker who doubled up as a cook and would serve us our choice of cooked Chinese food. Since we were frequent visitors, he came to know our culinary habits. Once, during the summer holidays, we stayed in this guest house for one month. My primary school-going two daughters ran up and down the beach and made sand castles. To avoid the sun's heat during the day, we spent a long time in the clean blue waters of the beach.

Figure 7.3. Beaches of Pangkor. **Upper:** Panoramic View of a Beach on the Malaysian Island of Pangkor (https://commons.wikimedia.org/wiki/File:Pangkor_Coral_Beach.jpg) by Michael C. This image is dedicated to the public domain under CC0 1.0 (https://creativecommons.org/publicdomain/zero/1.0/?ref=chooser-v1). **Lower Left:** Teluk Nipah (Nipah Bay in English) on the Western Side of Pangkor Island, in Malaysia (https://commons.wikimedia.org/wiki/File:Teluk_Nipah.jpg) by Michael C. This image is dedicated to the public domain under CC0 1.0 (https://creativecommons.org/publicdomain/zero/1.0/?ref=chooser-v1) **Lower Right:** Pasir Bogak, Pangkor Island, July 1976 (https://www.flickr.com/photos/193055396@N08/51745846141/) by Wilford Peloquin. This image is licensed under CC BY 2.0 (https://creativecommons.org/licenses/by/2.0/deed.en#). *Lower Left: Telok Nipah Beach.* Nipah's name is associated with the fatal Nipah virus. However, it is not Pangkor's Nipah town from where the first virus deaths were reported in 1998; it is from the city of Sungei Nipah in Port Dickson, Negri Sembilan state of Malaysia. Nipah, literally meaning river, is not an uncommon name in Malay. *Lower Right: Pasar Bogok Beach ,Pangkor.* It is a beautiful beach within walking distance from the Coral Bay beach—lovely white sands of the beach and crystal clear emerald green water. The beach has water sports facilities and is a veritable holiday resort which tourists cherish.'

Pangkor Island was reached by road, and my Volkswagon would cover 174 Km distance in about two hours. Most often, I visited Pangkor to entertain visitors from abroad. These visitors could be the external examiners visiting the department or my personal and family friends coming from around the world on holiday visits to Malaysia. We would travel by car from Kuala Lumpur (in the state of Selangor) to the ferry terminal town of Lumit (in the state of Perak) to board the ferry for Pangkor Island. The car was parked in Lumit, and the ferry journey would take 45 minutes. Pangkor had a beach-side Chalet Hotel and Bar with Chinese cuisine. We would stay at the comfortable Chalets, conveniently located near the beach.

The Dutch visited Pangkor Island in the 17th century CE. The ruins of their fort are still visible on the island.

Figure 7.4. **Left**: Puteri Beach, Tanjung Kling, Malacca, Malaysia (https://commons.wikimedia.org/wiki/File:Puteri_Beach.JPG) by Wikimedia user 'Chongkian'. This image is licensed under CC BY-SA 4.0 (https://creativecommons.org/licenses/by-sa/4.0/deed.en). **Right:** Desaru Beach, Desaru, beachfront resorts. There is also a nearby Ostriches farm with more than 100 Ostriches.Kota Tinggi, Johor, Malaysia (https://commons.wikimedia.org/wiki/File:Desaru_Beach.jpg) by Wikimedia user 'Chongkian'. This image is licensed under CC BY-SA 4.0 (https://creativecommons.org/licenses/by-sa/4.0/deed.en).

'*Puteri Beach Malacca*: The beach is located in Tanjung Kling. The beach had been developed as a resort beach. Various sports facilities are available, as well as fishing and camping. The beach area also has night markets, hotels, eateries, and restaurants along the road parallel to the shoreline. *Desaru Beach of Johar Baru.* The beach is located in the town of Desaru near fishing villages. It has Desaru Coast Adventure Waterpark., nature-based activities, and a few beachfront resorts. There is also a nearby Ostriches farm with more than 100 Ostriches.'

'*Teluk Cempedak Beach in Kuantan.* The beach, also known as Palm Beach, is close to the city centre of Kuantan. It offers a peaceful ambience, and the beach has clear waters for swimming. A food court and restaurant are present near the beach. *Kuala Terengganu Main Beach.* At *244* km, it is the longest beach in Malaysia, with breathtaking scenery, white powdery sand beaches, and crystal-clear water. The beach is a perfect blend of *Sun, Sand, and Sea. Perhentian Besar(Big) Island,* also called Turtle Beach. It is known for turtle preservation and wildlife reserves. The green turtles lay eggs at night when they are seen coming out of the sea.'

Pangkor is a tropical paradise with its pristine white sandy beaches and azure waters surrounded by lush green rainforests. It is a romantic, serene retreat from the hustle and bustle of city life. It allows guests to connect with the paradise of nature in a tranquil ambience. The beaches of Pangkor Island include Pasir Bogak, Teluk Nipah, and

Coral Beach. We visited these beaches on day tours from Pangkor.

Figure 7.5. Peninsula Malaysia, East Coast Beaches **Upper Left:** Photo Taken On The Bridge (https://commons.wikimedia.org/wiki/File:Teluk-cempedak-pantai.jpg) by Wikimedia user 'Sihyoong.' This image is licensed under CC BY-SA 4.0 (https://creativecommons.org/licenses/by-sa/4.0/deed.en). **Upper Right:** Beach at Kuala Terengganu,Malaysia(https://commons.wikimedia.org/wiki/File:Kuala_Terengganu,_Malaysia,_Main_beach.jpg) by Vyacheslav Argenberg (http://www.vascoplanet.com/). This image is licensed under CC BY 4.0 (https://creativecommons.org/licenses/by/4.0/deed.en). **Lower Left:** National Marine Park Boat, Pulau Perhentian Besar (https://commons.wikimedia.org/wiki/File:Perhentian_Besar,_Malaysia,_Marine_National_Park_Boat.jpg) by Vyacheslav Argenberg (http://www.vascoplanet.com/). This image is licensed under CC BY 4.0 (https://creativecommons.org/licenses/by/4.0/deed.en). **Lower Right:** Beach Pasir Panjang on Pulau Redang (https://commons.wikimedia.org/wiki/File:Pasir_Panjang.JPG) by Wikimedia user 'Singaporean'. This image is dedicated to the public domain.

Because of their proximity to Kuala Lumpur, we frequently visited Port Dickson and Pangkor Island beaches during weekends and local holidays.

The east coast of the Malaysian Peninsula is mainly rural. It offers some of the Peninsula's unspoiled islands and beaches and is excellent for scuba diving. There is a continuous row of white sandy beaches from the coast of Kuantan in the south to the coast of Kota Baru in the north. However, the most popular beaches are located on the shores of Kuantan, Kuala Terengganu, and Kota Baru.

Kuantan Beaches: Teluk Cempedak Beach, or Palm Beach, is the main sightseeing beach of Kuantan. However, other scenic beaches near the city are popular with holidaymakers: Batu Hitam, Balok, Chenor, Pantai Sepat, Beserah, and Cherating.

Kuala Terengganu: The Main Beach of Kuala Terengganu is the longest in Malaysia, 244 Km long. We visited this beach and stayed at the Government rest house near the beach.

There are several island beaches; the famous Pasir Panjang is in Pulau Redang. Other Island beaches include Turtle Sanctuary Beach, Perhentian Island Beach, Long Beach, Teluk Keke, Batu Burok Beach, Buit Kluang Beach, Telok Kalong Beach, Pantai Telok Bidara, and Kemask Beach.

Part II

Kuwait and the Arab Peninsula

Chapter 1

PENINSULA ARABS

The human race's ancestors can be traced to Africa, where they first separated from primates and then from archaic humans. The developed humans started leaving Africa by several coastal routes to different parts of the world. The southern route brought the initial migration of humans into the Arabian Peninsula millions of years back, leading to the transformation and development of the first Eurasian populations. References to Arab people have been recorded since the 9th century BCE. The present-day Arabs are thought to be the direct descendants of these ancient people. However, the old tradition holds that Arabs descend from Ishmael, the son of Abraham, and the Syrian desert is the home of the first attested "Arab" groups.

The early Arabs developed primarily as nomadic or Bedouins and settled pastoral population groups in the Arabian Peninsula, Syrian desert, and Mesopotamia. The settled agricultural populations located themselves in Yemen, south of the peninsula and along the borders with Syria and Iraq. The harsh interior was the domain of camel-raising nomads or Bedouins.

The Bedouins (Badawi, Bedouin, or desert people) constantly moved across the Arabian sands with animal flocks for water and food. The Bedouins evolved into a tribal structure that spread to settled communities. The settled people engaged in agriculture and laid the basis for oasis towns. The pre-Islamic peoples were mostly pagans with polytheistic religious structures, though monotheistic Jewish tribes also existed on the peninsula. With the arrival of Islam in the seventh century, the sacred structure changed, and almost all the people of Arabia professed Islam.

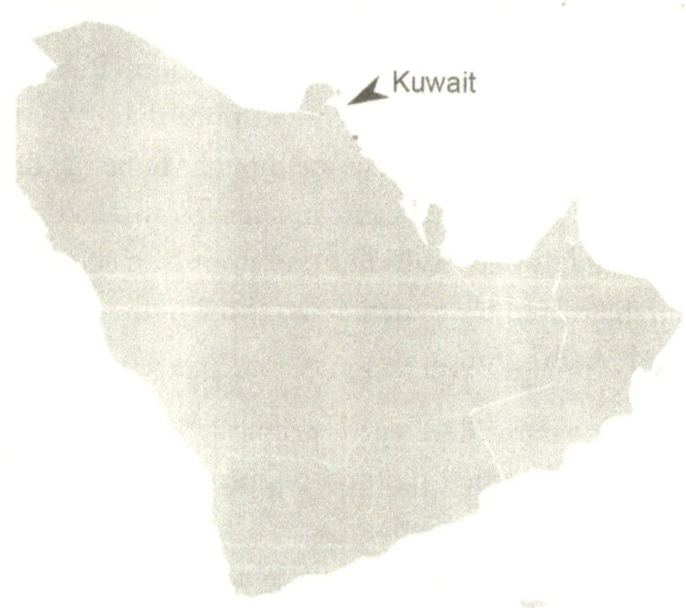

Figure 1.1. Sketch of the Arabian Peninsula.

Stradling along the east coast of the Peninsula are the independent states of Arabian Gulf countries: Kuwait at the tip of the Arabian Gulf and the islands of Bahrain and Qatar off the east coast. Oman and Yemen occupy the southern rim of the Peninsula. All these regions formed the Arab world, and the people became Arabs because of the spread of the Arabic language.

Later, Islamic conquests of the 7th and 8th centuries consolidated Arabs in these lands. The Arabs established the caliphates of Rashidun (632-661 CE), Umayyad (661-750 CE), and the Abbasid (750-1258 CE), constructing one of the largest land empires in history. The empire stretched from Morocco and other lands in North Africa, Egypt, Sudan, the Levant, and Arabia, spreading the Arabic language and Islamic culture and forging a much larger Arab World, though not an Arab Nation, the cherished dream of the idealists. Nevertheless, the Peninsular Arabs retained their ethnic Arab origin. Today, there are 22 independent sovereign Arabic-speaking countries in the world. The Arab population of these countries is urbanized, and most of the population is educated, though small groups of Bedouins still roam in the desert like their ancestors.

Figure 1.2. **Upper Left:** Bedoeïnen met hun schapen (Bedouins with their sheep) (http://hdl.handle.net/10648/aee437b4-d0b4-102d-bcf8-003048976d84) originally photographed by Willem van de Poll, copyright acquired by the National Archives, The Netherlands. This image is dedicated to the public domain under CC0 1.0 (https://creativecommons.org/publicdomain/zero/1.0/?ref=chooser-v1). Upper Right: A caravan crossing the Ad Dahna desert in central Saudi Arabia (https://commons.wikimedia.org/wiki/File:A_journey.jpg) by Mohammad Nowfal. This image is licensed under a Free Art License (http://artlibre.org/lal/en). Lower Left: A Tent Hamlet on the outskirts of Kuwait City. Kuwaitis recall their desert heritage by sleeping on the sand once a year. Courtesy Felix Pereria **Lower Right:** Interior of one of the Tents. Tent Hamlet images by Harris Felix Pereira.

I lived and worked in Kuwait for 30 years and have first-hand knowledge of these time-tested and hardened desert peoples. Bedouin society is tribal and male-dominated and composed of extended families. The head of the family and the larger tribal units is called the *Sheikh*, a respected senior man of the family and tribe. The

Bedouins are classified according to the animal species that form the basis of their livelihood. The Camel nomads are organized as large tribes and occupy large territories. Sheep and goat nomads have smaller territorial ranges and mostly stay near cultivated areas. Cattle nomads are found chiefly in Saudi Arabia and Sudan.

The honour code for Bedouins is hospitality, courage, and bravery, symbolizing manliness, loyalty to family, and pride in ancestry. They viciously protect and abide by the tenets of Islam and consider it as their heritage. Poetry reciting is the most famous art form in Bedoiuns. Having a poet in the tribe was highly regarded. Bedouin poetry follows the style of Najd, central Arabia, and is known as Nabati poetry, which is often recited in vernacular Arabic. Disputes among the tribes occur due to territorial aggression, stealing, particularly animals, and sometimes over the honour of women.

The urbanized Bedouins and the city dwellers reminiscence their desert heritage by staying in the desert during springtime every year. It was common to see several tents pitched up on the city's outskirts desert by Kuwaiti Arab residents and Bedouins of Kuwait City. The tents would have electricity and other electrical comfort appliances. By staying in the tents, they would replicate the lives of their ancestors and evoke their desert heritage.

Almost all Arabs adhere to Islam and its Sharia. A tiny percentage of Arabs are Christians. Saudi Arabia and Kuwait are conservative in their religious outlook, while the states of Bahrain, Qatar, Abu Dhabi, and Oman are liberal to a variable extent.

The Arab world countries, from Morocco to Iraq, share a common culture, traditions, language, and history that distinguishes these regions from other parts of the Islamic world.

Figure 1.3. **Left:** Palestinian girls dancing traditional Dabke (https:// commons.wikimedia.org/wiki/File:Palestinian_girls_dancing_traditional_ Dabke.jpg). jpg) by Sarah Canbel (Wikimedia user 'Sarah SchneiderCH'). This image is licensed under CC BY-SA 4.0 (https://creativecommons.org/ licenses/by-sa/4.0/deed.en).

Storytelling, music, and poetry reciting are long traditions in the Arab world. Arabic music is rich and has various styles and genres that vary from country to country. Each Arabic country has its traditional music. Although there is interaction with many regional music styles and genres, it did not evolve as a standard Arabic style. Some top singers have emerged recently and created classic Arabic, folk, and pop sounds enjoyed not only in Arab countries but also in the rest of the world. Umm Kulthum leads the list of these iconic singers. The melodious voice of Umm Kulthum has been pleasant to many ears, and I used to enjoy listening to her music and melodies even though I could understand little Arabic. Umm Kulthum has been called the 'Lata Mangeshkar of the Middle East.' Lata Mangeshkar was the most outstanding Indian singer, entertaining India and the world with thousands of classic melodies. Umm Kulthum died in 1975 at the age of 71. The other singer, Khaled, rendered a dancing musical hit, 'DiDi, 'which I enjoyed listening to back in the early nineties.

Figure 1.4. Monument to singer and musician Umm Kulthum (Oum Kalsoum) in Zamalek district, Gezira Island, in Cairo (https://commons. wikimedia.org/wiki/File:Oum_Kalsoum_Monument_Zamalek_Cairo_Jan-2006.jpg) by Błażej Pindor (Wikimedia user 'Blago Tebi'). This image is licensed under CC BY-SA 3.0 (https://creativecommons.org/licenses/by-sa/3.0/deed.en).

Figure 1.5. This is an image of dancer Layla Taj (https://commons. wikimedia.org/wiki/File:Layla_Taj_wikipedia_article.jpg) by Amos Gvili. This image is licensed under CC BY-SA 4.0 (https://creativecommons.org/ licenses/by-sa/4.0/deed.en)

Like the music, Arab dances have different styles: folklore, classical and contemporary. However, Arab *belly dancing* is the most popular style in Arabia and the rest of the world. In addition, *Ardah* and *Dabke* are also popular Arab dances.

Certain Sufi sects perform Sufi Whirling Dances or Dances of the Sufi Dervashas to achieve higher enlightenment and proximity to Allah by listening to music, focusing on Allah, and spinning one's body in repetitive circles through ecstatic religious dancing. The Sufi groups that practice these dances are of the Mevlevi order, Rifa'I Marufi order, and others. The whirling Dervishes order was introduced in the 13th century CE in Konya, Turkey, by Jalal al-Din Mohammad Rumi, known to his followers as Mevlena or Rumi. Rumi was influenced by the practices of the Greek monks who lived in the caves of monasteries near Konya and who had a tradition of hymn singing and dancing. The Mausoleum of Rumi and his family in Koyna, where the dancing dervish performs, is a major tourist attraction in Turkey.

Figure 1.6. Dances of Arabia. **Upper Left:** Arab dance of Shamadan (https://commons.wikimedia.org/wiki/File:SHAMADAN.jpg) by Sarah Canbel (Wikimedia user 'Sarah SchneiderCH'). This image is licensed under CC BYSA 4.0 (https://creativecommons.org/licenses/by-sa/4.0/deed.en). Upper Right: Arab girls dancing Khaleegy dance (https://commons.wikimedia.org/wiki/File:Arab_girls_dancing_Khaleegy_dance.jpg) by Sarah Canbel (Wikimedia user 'Sarah SchneiderCH'). This image is licensed under CC BYSA 4.0 (https://creativecommons.org/licenses/by-sa/4.0/deed.en). Lower Left: Mwald celebrations of the Prophet's family in Egypt (https://commons.wikimedia.org/wiki/File:Dance_in_Religious_concert.jpg) by Wikimedia user 'Mahmoud1Ibrahim'. This image is licensed under CC BY-SA 4.0 (https://creativecommons.org/licenses/by-sa/4.0/deed.en). Lower Right: Dance of the Dervishes (https://digi.ub.uniheidelberg.de/diglit/dodwell1821/0047/image,info) by Edward Dodwell. This image is in the public domain.

Kuwait developed indigenous theatrical traditions, and the first theatre in Kuwait and Arabian Gulf countries opened in the thirties of the last century. The first Cinema company, Kuwait National Cinema Company (KNCC), was opened in 1954. It was the first leading cinema company in Kuwait and the Gulf. The first cinemas, Al Hamra and Al Firdous, were built in the Sharq area around the same time.

The style of the dress worn by Arabs had not changed much since the 6ᵗʰ century CE when the formal Arab dress evolved to give protection against heat, dust, and blazing sunshine. A heavy long gown is worn in the winter, while a light long gown covering all body parts and up to the ankles is worn in the summer. The gown is variously called *jellaba* or *dishdashah*. Traditional clothing is also used mainly by city dwellers. The *aba or abaya* is of ancient origin and is mentioned as the attire of the Hebrew prophets. Both sexes wear traditional loose, baggy trousers.

The customary male headdress is a kaffiyeh, a square of white or patterned cloth folded into a triangle and placed on the head, the two ends falling on the shoulders and the third at the back of the head. The fabric is held in place by the *agal,* a corded band decorated with beads or threads. Footwear for both sexes is usually in the form of sandals.

The tradition for women to cover themselves from head to toe is an ancient tradition predating Islam in Iran and other regional countries. The enveloping cloaks worn by women, called burka, chador, or chadri, have a mesh panel through which the women can peer into the outside world.

Most city dwellers, men and women, wear modern dresses, though they change to traditional clothing when visiting family or friends and on ceremonial occasions. Most women cover their heads outside their houses with clothes and wear long, regular dresses. The burqa is seen in the Arab world, though it is very common in Afghanistan and some societies in the Indian subcontinent.

Social visits by friends and acquaintances to the houses are segregated, with separate areas for men and women called *Dewaniya*. Dewaniya is an ancient tradition in the countries of the Middle East predating Islam.

Figure 1.7. Traditional Arab Dresses. **Upper Left:** Assorted Arabs (https://www.flickr.com/photos/marypaulose/) by Flickr User 'Oman Muscat'. This image is licensed under CC BY 2.0 (https://creativecommons.org/licenses/by/2.0/deed.en). Upper Right: Waiting - Herat, Afghanistan (https://www.flickr.com/photos/anarkistix/4112238624/) by Marius Arnesen. This image is licensed under CC BY-SA 2.0 (https://creativecommons.org/licenses/by-sa/2.0/deed.en.

The reception room is in a separate part of the house, where male friends and family gather and exchange news and views. Sweets are served on special occasions; sometimes, dinner is offered. Dewaniya is a place for quick communication and consensus-building on public matters and important government decisions. It is also a place for concluding business deals and resolving disputes.

Arab cuisine has developed over the centuries, mostly uniform, with some regional variations. The central part of the daily food is rice and leavened bread made of fermented dough. The bread is baked in the earthen oven. There are many types of sauces (sibagh) which survived from ancient times, including chickpeas sauce and homos. Fasulia (beans curry with meats) and bamia (Okhra curry with meats) are typical vegetable dishes. All types of meats are used, but the preferred ones are goat meat and chicken. Kebabs and Shawarna are the primary meat preparations relished.

Chapter 2

KUWAIT AND KUWAITI PEOPLE

The ancient lands of Kuwait, situated at the tip of the Arabian Gulf, were the central site for interaction between the people of Mesopotamia and Eastern Arabia. The lands of Kuwait have been continuously inhabited since 2000 BCE. During its pre-Christ history, Kuwait was occupied by Sumerians, Dilmun, and Babylonians. Northern Kuwait and Failaka Island served as the seats of these civilizations. The Achaemenid empire of Persia colonized the Bay of Kuwait in the 6th century BCE and the Greeks in the 4th century BCE. Alexander the Great named mainland Kuwait *Larissa,* and the Failaka was named *Ikaros* because it resembled the Greek island of the same shape.

The origin of Kuwait and its modern history are generally believed to have started at the beginning of the 18th century CE when the Bani Utub, a group of families from the Anizah tribe of the Peninsula, began migrating to the area that now forms the State of Kuwait. The families established the city-state and appointed a Sheikh from one of the families, the Al-Sabah family. The descendants of this family have ruled the State of Kuwait ever since. The Al Sabah family adheres to the Maliki school of Sunni Islam.

The Kuwaiti people developed into successful business people, and business flourished between Mesopotamia in the north and the eastern Arabian peninsula. They created large ocean-going boats (dhows) and established overseas trade with the west coast of India, the east coast of Africa, and as far as Singapore, becoming maritime traders. Kuwaitis became an independent, thriving trading and predominantly sea-faring community. It was the centre of dhows building in the Persian Gulf region, and its sailors set a positive reputation in the Gulf and the Indian Ocean. In the 19th century CE, Kuwait developed a significant horse trade and exported Arabian horses mainly to India.

The Al-Sabah family ruled the tiny State of Kuwait. Pre-oil, the family established the Sheikhdom of Kuwait. Towards the end of the 19th century CE, Sheikh Mubarak al Kabir emerged as a strong ruler and became the Amir of Kuwait. He faced the challenges of two dominant powers, The Ottoman Empire and the British Empire, casting their shadows on the sands of the Arabian Peninsula. Sheikh Mubarak allied with the British to remove the Ottoman threat to annexe Kuwait. In 1899, a treaty with the British, granted control of Kuwait's foreign affairs in exchange for thwarting Ottoman ambitions. After the end of WWI, Kuwait became a British protectorate.

Figure 2.1. Sketch Map of Kuwait.

Sheikh Mubarak built the iconic Seif Palace in 1904 as the seat of the government. The top of the clock tower is covered in pure gold plate. Seif Palace was built in three extensions.

With the growing influence and hegemony of the British in the Persian Gulf region, the Ottoman Empire, during the 1913-14 negotiations, agreed to the British demand, recognized British control over Kuwait, which was considered part of the Ottoman province of Basrah, and decided to demarcate Kuwait's northern border with Iraq which was finally done in 1922.

Figure 2.2. Sheikh Mubarak Al-Sabah of Kuwait (https://commons. wikimedia.org/wiki/File:Mubarak_Al-Sabah_of_Kuwait.jpg) by Hermann Burchardt. This image is in the public domain.

The British also demarcated the borders of Kuwait with neighbouring Saudi Arabia. While the Saudi border agreement was ratified with significant loss of territory to Kuwait, the border with Iraq remained unratified. Iraq put forward claims for the two strategic islands of Kuwait, Bubiyan and Al-Warbah. These claims were repeated when oil was discovered in Kuwait in 1938. To strengthen Kuwait's position, Britain recognized Kuwait's independence in 1961. The British and the Arab League rebuffed the Iraqi claims. It was not until 1963 that the new Iraqi regime formally recognized Kuwait's sovereignty and its borders, but Iraq continued to press for the islands. Persistent claims over Kuwait by Iraq were one of the factors which precipitated the Gulf War of 1990.

Between 1900 and 1990, Kuwait successfully dealt with several disputes and skirmishes: the Kuwait-Rashidi War (1900-1901), the Battle of Jo-Laban (1903), the Battle of Hadia (1910), the Mesopotamian Campaign (1914-1918), the Kuwait-Najd War (1919-1920), Battle of Jahra (1920), Ikhwan Revolt (1927-1930), Six Days War (1967), Samita Border Skirmish (1973), the October War (1973), the Invasion of Kuwait(1990), and the Gulf War(1990-1991). Incredibly, the people of this tiny state, with sheer grit and determination, faced and thwarted all these challenges to their survival as independent people for almost 200 years.

During my extended stay in Kuwait, I dealt with and observed Kuwaiti people closely at all levels of society. Kuwaiti society transformed from the lower middle and poor class status of the pre-oil days to a rich and super-rich status after the discovery of oil. This transformation of society has been phenomenal.

This fast development significantly affected social and communal behaviour, the general outlook of living, and attitudes towards expatriate communities. With the general improvement of household income, luxuries and comforts poured in, and household helpers, mainly from South Asian countries, became a norm and a social status. These maids, from the lowest rung of South Asian societies, doing menial household work created the first impression of South and Southeast Asian people, which stuck in the minds of the Kuwaitis. The Kuwaitis, in general, started painting the expatriates, educated, professionals or otherwise, with the same brush. It brought exclusiveness and, at times, arrogance to the outlook of Kuwaitis, affluent, academic, or otherwise, when dealing with most expatriates. This subconscious attitude prevented the ingress of the expatriates into Kuwaiti society. Human-to-human friendships did develop, and there were plenty of them, but the inherent prejudices remained. It was extremely rare to see matrimonial alliances between expatriates and Kuwaitis. The relationships were mostly business-like.

Kuwaitis, like their other Arab counterparts, respect learning and learned people, and their religious injunction encourages them to do so. The Kuwaiti people welcomed and honoured expatriate educated professionals, who were generally eager to learn and take advantage of their experiences in education, healthcare, business, and other areas. They socialize with the expatriates and invite them to their houses for food and sometimes drinks. These dinner meetings are more like a male dewaniya, and the lady of the house is most often not seen. They remain secluded in the house. In the Arab world, socialization remains mostly a male-dominated event.

A recent survey (16 personalities.com) about the personality profiles of Kuwaitis found some interesting features: Kuwaitis tend to be more extroverted, less observant and thinkers, less judgemental, and less assertive but more turbulent. These profiles indicate Kuwaiti people are more prone to impulsive behaviour.

Kuwait has an estimated population of 4.25 million, according to the 2019 census. Approximately 70% of this population is expatriates from almost 100 countries of the world. About 60% of the total population is Arab, which includes Arab expatriates. The largest expat communities are Egyptians and Indians. The communities live virtually in compartments with little social and cultural interaction.

The Kuwaiti population, which is predominantly Arab, displays several class divisions. The anchor of Kuwaiti society is the 'family' around which life revolves. The family is hierarchical, and the first family of Kuwait is the Al-Sabah family, which has been providing rulers (Amirs) of Kuwait for the past two hundred years. Other families follow from there regarding their relative social and economic status and importance in society. Social interaction and matrimonial alliances are made with near equal status of the families. But nowadays, with the city-dwelling educated elite, such social barriers are easily overcome.

Though Kuwaiti society has been raised to a higher material level with the discovery of oil, there are social, cultural, and sectarian divisions within the citizen groups. Another contributory factor is the entry of several working-class and business people from the neighbouring countries, who became non-citizens and permanent residents but did not enjoy any social benefits. Benefits typically permeated the citizen groups.

In the pre-oil days, Kuwait did not develop its ports for commercial activity but relied on the Iranian ports in its proximity. Business people started coming to Kuwait, mainly from neighbouring Iran. Marafi Behbehani was one of the first Iranian merchants to settle in Kuwait in the 18th century CE, and more followed. These Iranian merchants were called *Ajam* merchants. Some Kuwaiti *Ajam* are of Sayyed descent, especially those from the Al-Musawi family. These merchants (Sunni and Shia) established themselves in the Sharq district of the old Kuwait city. This group preserved the Persian language and culture and remained isolated in the otherwise Arabic-speaking Kuwait City. They found the first trade centre in Kuwait, the *Old Souk or Souk Al-Mubarakeya*. This market has been in Kuwait for almost 200 years. The market has several consumer goods and accessories shops and gold and silver jewellery shops. Kuwait and other Gulf states are lucrative markets for this yellow metal because of its purity and competitive prices. The other attractions are the Persian silk carpets, Arab antiques, perfumes, and traditional costumes.

Figure 2.3. Old Souk of Kuwait. **Left:** Al-mubarakeya market in Kuwait City, one of the oldest markets in Kuwait City(https://commons.wikimedia. org/wiki/File:Elmubarakiya-market-kuwait.jpg) by Wikimedia User 'Aziz1005'. This image is in the public domain. Right: The date seller is in the old souq in Kuwait City, surrounded by dates from Kuwait, Iran, and Saudi Arabia. Arabia and elsewhere (https://commons.wikimedia.org/wiki/ File:Date-seller.jpg) by Trammell Hudson (Wikimedia user 'Autopilot'). This image is licensed under CC BY-SA 3.0 (https://creativecommons.org/ licenses/by-sa/3.0/).

After the discovery of oil and the development of oil-based industries, the *Ajam* groups relocated to more affluent neighbourhoods. It was the time when they started mixing with local Arabs and learning their language and customs. It was easy for the Sunni Iranians to integrate into Kuwaiti society, but Iranian Shia protected their religion, customs, and ethics privately. Today, Iranian Kuwaitis dress, talk, and behave like native Kuwaitis in public, though sometimes they betray their Iranian identity.

Figure 2.4. Liberation Tower in the Evening (https://commons. wikimedia.org/wiki/File:Liberation_Tower._Kuwait.jpg) by Wikimedia user 'Anielparur.' This image is licensed under CC BY-SA 4.0 (https:// creativecommons.org/licenses/by-sa/4.0/deed.en).

The *Ajam* merchants started the modernization of Kuwait. Yusuf Behbehani opened the first hotel in Kuwait. M. Ma'arafie imported the first refrigerator in Kuwait, operated the first telephone in Kuwait, and opened the first radio agency in Kuwait in the thirties of the last century. Murad Behbehani started the first television (black and white) in Kuwait in 1961 and later introduced colour television in 1974. He founded Kuwait Television, KTV, which was subsequently nationalized.

The *Ajam* community's culinary traditions enriched Kuwait's cuisine. *Ajam* is known for bread making, and the earthen oven-baked Iranian bread is a treat. We used to enjoy this bread often when in Kuwait. The Iranian Zubadi fish is a staple food. Other traditional Iranian-based *Ajam* dishes include Ghormesh or Khorest sabzi, which is made up of beans and meat and is very popular and Iran's national dish. *Ajam* dishes of nakhi and bajella are equally relished.

Over the years, several other big business houses mushroomed in Kuwait, which brought hectic commercial activity and the economic and physical development of the city. High-rises and skyscrapers have recently appeared in the city, changing its skyline. The business-based economy flourished and, complementary to the oil-based economy, transformed Kuwait City into a modern metropolis.

Oil was commercially discovered in Kuwait in 1938, and the first oil well was installed in the Burgan area of southeastern Kuwait. Greater Burgan, consisting of Burgan, Magwa, and Ahmadi oil fields, produces around 1.6 million barrels per day. The country has an estimated 9 billion barrels of proven oil reserves. However, after almost 85 years of oil exploitation, the stress on the oil fields is evident, which may be causing concern to the policy planners in Kuwait.

Figure 2.5. Kuwait City Skyline in 2008. Downtown Kuwait City Skyline (https://www.flickr.com/photos/robef/8016482071/) by Rob Faulkner. This image is licensed under CC BY 2.0 (https://creativecommons.org/licenses/by/2.0/deed.en#).

Figure 2.6. Oil Well and the Pumpjack. A Representative picture. A pumpjack in Texas (https://commons.wikimedia.org/wiki/File:Oil_well.jpg) by Wikimedia user 'Flcelloguy.' This image is licensed under CC BY-SA 3.0 (https://creativecommons.org/licenses/by-sa/3.0/).

There is no semblance of any significant social or cultural interaction between the Kuwaitis and the expatriate communities, mostly floating communities. It was easy for the Muslim expatriates to interact religiously with the locals, and Christian Churches were permitted to operate. However, non-Muslim,non-Christian expatriate groups were handicapped to practice their religion publically and build their places of worship in Kuwait. One of the major expatriate groups in Kuwait is the Indian group, which is almost a million in number. Most Indians adhere to Hinduism, Islam, or Sikhism. Hindus and Sikhs practice their religious obligations in the privacy of their homes. Only 'Religions of the Book' can.

Chapter 3

NATION BUILDING

Nation-building processes require a steady availability of educated cadres to run the country's political, economic, security, and social institutions. To impart higher education to the high school leavers, Kuwait University was established in 1966 and was housed on the Shuwaikh Campus facing Kuwaiti Bay. The university had Colleges of Science and Humanities and a women's college. Later, six more campuses were established, the largest being the Khaldiya Campus, with most of the university colleges and university administration relocated there.

Figure 3.1. **Left:** Khaldiya Campus (https://commons.wikimedia.org/wiki/File:Khaldiya_Campus.JPG) by Wikimedia user 'Kuwait University.' This image is licensed under CC BY-SA 4.0 (https://creativecommons.org/licenses/by-sa/4.0/deed.en). Right: Shuwaikh Campus (https://commons.wikimedia.org/wiki/File:Shuwaikh_Campus.jpg) by Wikimedia user 'Kuwait University.' This image is licensed under CC BY-SA 4.0 (https://creativecommons.org/licenses/by-sa/4.0/deed.en

Figure 3.2. Deans (Top) and Vice-Deans (Right) of the Faculty of Medicine. Courtesy: Professor Hussain Dashti.

The Health Sciences Centre (HSC) of Kuwait University was established in 1982 as the governing institution of the existing faculties of Medicine, Allied Health Sciences, Dentistry, and Pharmacy. It is headed by a Vice President, a council of deans of faculties, and co-opted members. Its role is to streamline the teaching of all faculties, which is a supervisory role.

Figure 3.3. **Left:** Faculty of Medicine, Jabriya Campus, Kuwait University, Kuwait, 1983. **Right:** Faculty of Medicine, temporary location at Shuwaikh Campus, Kuwait University. The image shows the staff and students of the Physiology Department in 1982.Personal Collection.

The Faculty of Medicine was established in 1973 and housed at its temporary location in the Shuwaikh campus. After completing two years of the premedical program in the science faculty, the students enrolled for the first preclinical program at the medical faculty. When I joined the department in 1980, the fourth batch of students was getting lessons in medical physiology. The chairman of the department was Dr A.C. Brown, an American physiologist. The senior Kuwaiti academic in the department was Prof. Naji Al-zaid (Sadly, Prof. Naji Al-Zaid passed away on January 01,2024 from natural causes). There were two academics from Sudan, and I was the only one from India. Initially, eighty students were enrolled for a five-year bachelor's program. Kuwait Medical Faculty was one of the earliest medical schools established in the Arabian Gulf region.

Figure 3.4. Professor Naji Al-Zaid, (Jan 15, 1948- Jan 01,2024). Courtesy Prof. Hussain Dashti.

The founding dean of the faculty was Prof. Abdulmoshin Yousef Al-Abdul Razaaqq, who belonged to the well-established and respected Abdul Razzaqq family of Kuwait. Professor Abdul-Razaqq, a British-trained cardiologist, practised medicine in the Ministry of Health in Kuwait since 1963 before becoming Head of the Amiri Hospital and later Head of the Cardiology, Chest Diseases Hospital in Kuwait. He also guided the destiny of Kuwait University as its President. His mandate was to establish the medical academic institution par-excellence, incorporating the best available medical academics from all over the world; to train medical graduates to a high level of competence capable of competing with the best compatriates in the world and of laying the foundation of high-quality research and providing incentives to the academic staff to develop state-of-the-art research laboratories.

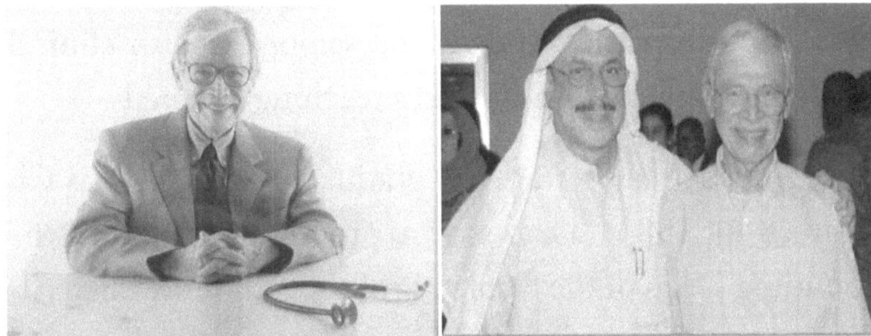

Figure 3.5. **Left:** Professor Abdulmoshin Yousof Al-Abdul Razaaqq, Founding Dean of the Faculty of Medine and former President of Kuwait University. **Right:** Professor Hussain Dashti posing with Professor Al-Razaaqq.Courtesy Professors AM Yousof and Hussain Dashti.

He further strengthened this vision by creating an ideal and harmonious environment with unrestrained working conditions that encouraged lively interpersonal relationships among academics from diverse countries. He introduced the subject-based medical education model, selected the staff, and developed the departments accordingly. He succeeded admirably in fulfilling all these objectives and left a rich legacy still being nurtured.

The faculty developed its full potential when it shifted to the new permanent building at the Jabryia campus in 1983. Across the road from the faculty was the Mubarak Al-Kabir Hospital, a major Kuwait city hospital run by the Ministry of Health and used as the primary teaching hospital for the faculty, along with other specialized Ministry hospitals scattered across the city. In later years, I supervised teaching at the department level as Chairman and the faculty level as vice-dean academic. The faculty attracted qualified senior staff from many countries of the world. Professor Moshin negotiated a special deal with Swedish universities, and several senior Swedish clinical academics appeared in Kuwait's teaching hospitals.

The first batch of students graduated with B.M.B.Ch degrees in 1983. That was a proud moment for the founding Dean of the faculty, Professor Abdulmoshen Al-Abdulrazaaq, who nurtured the faculty and worked hard to see that day. A total of 2434 students have completed the five-year program till 2019.

Figure 3.6. **Left:** Dean Abdullatif Al-Bader. **Right:** Dean Al-Bader, surrounded by his Vice-Deans, chairing the Faculty Council meeting. Courtesy Professor Abdullatif Al-Bader.

Dean Abdullatif Al-Bader took over from Professor Moshin and continued the faculty's development. He took measures to boost the research activities of the academic staff. Research funding and resources were adequately provided to the academic staff and the graduate students. In due course, the quality and quantity of published research in international journals increased significantly, a measure of excellence for any medical school. Impressed with this accomplishment, the regional peers rated the faculty as the best medical school east of the Mediterranean.

Figure 3.7. **Upper Left:** Faculty of Dentistry, Kuwait University. **Upper Right:** Faculty of Allied Health Sciences. **Lower Left:** Faculty of Pharmacy, Kuwait University, Kuwait.

Graduate programs at master's and doctoral levels were introduced in all the disciplines of pre-clinical sciences. In collaboration with the Royal Colleges of England and Royal Australasian Colleges, the clinical departments introduced fellowship examinations for these colleges.

Faculties of Allied Health Sciences(1982), Dentistry (1996), and Pharmacy (1997) were established alongside the campus of the Faculty of Medicine, which shaped the Health Sciences Centre (HSC) of Kuwait University. A recent addition to the HSC was the Faculty of Public Health. To honour the founding dean of the medical faculty, the centre was named *Abdulmohsen Al-Abdulrazaaq Health Sciences Centre.*

Figure 3.8. Health Sciences Centre, Kuwait Unversity, Kuwait.

My association with Kuwait started In April of 1980 when I was offered the job of a full professor at the Faculty of Medicine of Kuwait University after completing all the appointment formalities. I resigned from my job in Kuala Lumpur, Malaysia. My wife and two school-going daughters accompanied me, and we landed in Kuwait at midnight on August 31, 1980. The university staff received us and brought us to the newly furnished apartment in the city. I joined the department housed in temporary accommodation at the Shuwaikh Campus and got involved in the department's activities from day one. Although I developed make-shift research facilities at Shuwaikh, my full research potential was realized after shifting to the newly built faculty campus at Jabriya. The offices and the attached laboratories were spacious, of contemporary design, and fully furnished, which acted as an inspiration to the working spirit. After almost thirty years of stay, my students from earlier batches stood shoulder-to-shoulder with me as full professors and colleagues, which was gratifying.

Since Kuwaiti-qualified medical academics to fill all the positions of the staff of newly established faculties of the HSC were not available, senior academics were hired from abroad. At one point, staff from almost one hundred countries contributed to Kuwait's nation-building activities. There was a healthy interaction between the diverse group of academics and the academics and students of various faculties. The culture and traditions of the expatriate groups penetrated Kuwaiti society through informal social interactions.

To maintain international standards of medical training, external examiners from different countries came every year to evaluate the students of all the faculties of the health science centre. There was also frequent exchange of visiting professors from abroad, primarily to monitor the research activities of the staff, provide input to improve the existing research of the staff and interact with the graduate students of the departments. External examiners examined graduate students' theses to attest to their international standing.

Chapter 4

SOCIAL AND CULTURAL LIFE

The social lives of the Kuwaiti people, like most Middle Eastern and Eastern societies, revolve around their extended families and children. Kuwaitis are family-oriented people who are proud of their family heritage. The family name determines the status of the Kuwaitis in society. There are strong bonds within the family. Bedouins remain at the tail end of the social status and are considered a group apart. The highest-status family in the land is the Al-Sabah family, the ruling family of Kuwait. The Kuwaitis are disciplined people who accept and respect the ruling hierarchy that has been ruling them for two hundred years.

Like Malaysians, Kuwaitis also develop social circles with friends and families. *Dewaniyas*, a great tradition among the Kuwaitis, are the places to socialize informally, where they meet with friends and families and greet each other on all occasions. Religious festivals are celebrated among families and friends in a simple and dignified way according to their religious injunction. Prayers are offered in the mosques during religious occasions, and families socialize over food and sweets.

Kuwaiti men and women have a peculiar greeting pattern of kissing. The left hand is extended to the other person's right shoulder while leaning, giving three kisses on either right-left-right or all on one cheek. It provides enough time to smell each other's cheeks. 'Sniff kiss' originated with the evolution of mankind. Early humans are thought to recognize each other by smell, developing the practice of 'sniff kiss.' Incredibly, the Middle Eastern people preserved this evolutionary practice of mankind, which was refined over the millenniums to the modern style. Most Kuwaiti men spray perfumes over their body and face to create a better 'sniff kiss.' There is a lucrative business in perfumes in Kuwait, and the best and most expensive brands of French perfumes are sought after. Most Kuwaitis greet each other by kissing. They welcome non-Kuwaities with a conventional handshake.

The people of Kuwait love art and patronize artistic values. They love music, dance, theatre, cinema, literature, and contemporary art. Islam influences Arab culture and traditions, which lay the foundation of the State of Kuwait. They popularised modern music in the Gulf, and the Kuwaitis were the first commercial recording artists. The discovery of oil did not change the essential character and identity of the Kuwaiti people, though they became more affluent, enjoying luxuries and living an opulent lifestyle. Old maritime mercantile tradition and nautical heritage, where Kuwaiti merchants, sailors, and pearl divers spent most of their lives, encouraged the origin and development of Kuwaiti music and dance. *Sawat* music, developed by the sea-faring Kuwaitis, has regional recognition. The famous song *Fidjeri* is a musical collection traditionally performed by pearl divers. *Liva* is another song from the African-origin Kuwaiti seafaring community. However, the most famous music of the Kuwaiti sailors is *al-Arda al-Bahariya,* as well as the song called *al-Nahma.*

Figure 4.1. Sheikh Jaber Al Ahmad Cultural Centre (also known as Kuwait Opera House) (https://commons.wikimedia.org/wiki/File:Jacckuwait.jpg) by Wikimedia user 'Tirimy.' This image is licensed under CC BY-SA 4.0 (https://creativecommons.org/licenses/bysa/4.0/deed.en).

Kuwait developed indigenous theatrical traditions, and the first theatre in Kuwait and Arabian Gulf countries opened in the thirties of the last century. The first Cinema company, Kuwait National Cinema Company (KNCC), was opened in 1954. It was the first leading cinema company in Kuwait and the Gulf. The first cinemas, Al Hamra and Al Firdous, were built in the Sharq area around the same time.

In recent years, Kuwait established a new National Cultural District (KNCD), the largest in the world, and consists of various venues for cultural activities, including Sheikh Abdulla Al-Salem Cultural Centre, Sheikh Jaber Al-Ahmad Cultural Centre, Al-Shaheed Park, and Al-Salam Palace.

Abdulla Al-Salem Cultural Centre is the largest museum complex in the Middle East.

A state–of–the–art *Sheikh Jaber Al-Ahmad Cultural Centre* was unveiled in 2016. The building is an architectural marvel. The modernistic cultural complex includes theatres, concert halls, music centres, conference halls, exhibition halls, cinemas, libraries, repositories of historical documents, public parks, and fountains.

Al-Shaheed Park is the largest urban park in Kuwait. The park includes various gardens, walkways, museums, exhibition spaces, and outdoor theatres for cultural events. In addition, there is a skate park, youth complex, and open-air performance venues. Several green-roofed buildings sit atop the park. It is one of the most extensive overstructured green roofs in the world.

Al-Salam Palace was commissioned by Amir Sheikh Abdullah Al-Salam Al-Sabah in the 1960s as his residence. However, after independence, the need arose for a guest house for international visitors, and AL-Salam Palace construction was completed instead of a royal palace, a royal guest house. More than 160 world leaders have stayed in this guest house since its opening in 1964. The world leaders who stayed included the Shah of Iran, Valery Giscard d'Estaing, the French President, Charles and Diana, Prince and Princess of Wales, and Indira Gandhi, Prime Minister of India.

Performing arts is an old tradition in Kuwait. Kuwait has developed training facilities in performing arts and scenographic education and is the only one in the Gulf. Kuwait also has a dedicated institute, The Higher Institute of Theatrical Arts, which imparts advanced training in theatrical arts.

Kuwait promoted the training in *modern arts* as early as 1936 and started a scholarship program for prospective candidates to be trained abroad. Mojeb al-Dousari was the first such scholar trained and the only one in the Arabian Gulf region then. The Sultan Gallery of Kuwait was the first established professional Arab art gallery in the Gulf.

Several museums in Kuwait preserve the history and culture of the region. The most prominent are the National Museum of Kuwait, the Modern Art Museum, the Scientific Centre, the Sadu House, and the Bait Al-Othman Museum.

Figure 4.2. The National Museum in Kuwait (https://en.wikipedia.org/wiki/File:Kuwait_Towers_RB.jpg) by Ahmad Al-Shami (Wikimedia user 'Kuwaitsoccer'). This image is licensed under CC BYSA. 3.0 (https://creativecommons.org/licenses/by-sa/3.0/).

Kuwait National Museum was established in 1983. It has three parts: the Failaka Island Hall, the Coin Hall, and the Cultural Hall. These museums display the history and culture of Kuwait and its ancient heritage. Modern Art Museum shows the history of art in Kuwait and the region. The Scientific Centre is one of the largest science museums in the Middle East. *Sadu House* was established by Al Sadu Society in 1980 to protect the interests of the Bedouins and their ethnic handicrafts, particularly Sadu weaving. Bait Al-Othman specializes in the History of Kuwait.

The Kuwait Maritime Museum preserves the country's maritime heritage. Kuwaitis have been seafaring mercantile communities from ancient to modern times, and the museum displays this heritage, notably by building ocean-going ships called *Dhows*. Kuwaitis have exclusive expertise in dhow building. Two prominent dhows, Fateh Al-Khayr and Al-Hashemi-II, entered the Guinness Book of World Records as the largest wooden dhows ever built. *Fateh Al-Khayr* is a 226-ton dhow, now preserved as a museum ship, built in 1938 in Kuwait by Abdul Rasool for the business houses of Mohammad Al-Ghanim and Thunayan Al-Ghanim. *Al-Hashemi-II* is the largest wooden ship in the world today, and it was built for 30 million dollars. It was commissioned by Husain Marafie, an eminent business family of Kuwait, in 1997. The dhow has never been floated on the high seas.

Figure 4.3. Historic Dhows of Kuwait. **Left:** Restored Dhow Fatah al Khair (2),(https://www.flickr.com/photos/110608682@N04/41238271364/) by Hans Birger Nilsen. This image is licensed under CC BY-SA 2.0 (https://creativecommons.org/licenses/bysa/2.0/deed.en). Right: The Kuwaiti Al-Hashemi-II, the largest dhow ever built (https://commons.wikimedia.org/wiki/File:Al-Hashemi-II_(ship).jpg) by Wikimedia user 'Mosbatho'. This image is licensed under CC BY 4.0 (https://creativecommons.org/licenses/by/4.0/deed.en).

Several museums in Kuwait are devoted to Islamic culture: Tareq Rajab Museums, a private enterprise, was established in 1980 and housed a fifty-year collection of artefacts by Tareq and Jehan Rajab. One of the museums is exclusively devoted to Islamic calligraphy. Dar al Athar al Islamiyah cultural centres include education wings, conservation labs, and research libraries.

Many of the museums in Kuwait are private enterprises and are supported by private families and groups. The civil society of Kuwait is to be lauded for its strength and entrepreneurial spirit in creating public cultural edifices in Kuwait.

The *major festivals* celebrated in Kuwait are New Year's Day, Liberation Day, National Day, Hala Festival, Ramadan, Eid el-Fitr, Eid el-Adha, Laylat ul Isra and Miraj, Mawlid an-Nabi and Islamic New Year.

Eid el-Fitr begins a day after the last day of *Ramadan*, the fasting month, and the celebrations last three days. When the sun sets on the last day of Ramadan, the new crescent of the moon is spotted, and this marks the start of Eid the following day, and the Kuwaitis and Muslims around the world feast. Muslims also visit mosques and say the Eid prayer; food and drinks are served there.

Eid el-Adha (*The Feast of Sacrifice*) is celebrated when the prophet *Abraham* prepared to sacrifice his son, *Ishmail*, to show his loyalty to God. At the last moment, God told Abraham that this was simply a test and that he did not have to sacrifice his son for Him. The Muslims celebrate this event by sacrificing an animal, usually a goat, in His honour to show their gratitude to Allah for saving Abraham's son's life. The sacrificed animal's meat is split into three portions and distributed traditionally: one for the man who sacrificed the animal, one for the man's poor relatives, and one for poor people in general, irrespective of race or religion.

Mawlid an-Nabi or the 'Birth of the Prophet.' Prophet Muhammad's birthday is celebrated on the twelfth day of the month of Rabi Al-Awal. Prayers to both Allah and Prophet Mohammad are offered on this day. Religious poetry is also chanted.

Laylat ulIsra and Miraj, meaning the '*the night of Power and Ascension.*' Isra is the first phase, where Prophet Muhammad journeyed from the Masjid al-Haram in Mecca horizontally to Masjid al-Aqsa (Jerusalem), and the second phase is the Ascension (Miraj), where he ascended vertically from al-Aqsa to heaven. Here, Prophet Muhammad and Allah talked about how many prayers should be said daily.

Ramadan Fasting. Ramadan is the 9th month of the Islamic calendar. This month, all Muslims are ordained to observe a complete fast and no eating or drinking after the sun has risen. They are permitted to break the fast once the sun goes down. The dates for Ramadan change yearly because the Islamic calendar is lunar.

Figure 4.4. Jerusalem, the Dome of the Rock, and the Western Wall (https://commons.wikimedia.org/wiki/File:Jerusalem_Dome_of_the_rock_BW_13.JPG) by Berthold Werner. This image is in the public domain.

Figure 4.5. Grosse Moschee Kuwait, Aussenansicht (https://commons. wikimedia.org/wiki/File:GrandMosqueKuwait.jpg) by Wikimedia user 'Mhp1255'. This image is licensed under CC BY-SA 4.0 (https:// creativecommons.org/licenses/by-sa/4.0/deed.en). Grand Mosque of Kuwait.

Gargee'an is a hundreds-year-old social tradition in Kuwait, and it takes place between the 13th and the 15th nights of Ramadan. The children in their best clothes go door to door in their neighbourhoods to receive sweets and sing traditional folk songs. The tradition is strikingly similar to the Indian Punjabi bonfire festival of *Lohri,* which is celebrated during the peak of winter on the 13th of January every year. Two to three days before the start of the festival, children, carrying dry branches of trees (symbolic fodder for bonfire) and singing the Lohri special song, '*Sunder Mundriye- Ho,*' go from door to door in their neighbourhoods and receive money (small change) and sweets.

HAJJ is the annual pilgrimage to Mecca, Saudi Arabia, and Islam's fifth pillar. The first pillar, *Profession of Faith (Shahada),* is the belief that " *There is no God but God and Muhammad is the Messenger of God,"* which is central to Islam. The second pillar is *Prayer (Salat).* The third pillar is *Alms (Zakat).* The fourth pillar is *Fasting (Sawn).* Hajj (Pilgrimage), the fifth pillar, is the largest annual pilgrimage in the world. It is a religious obligation that should be carried out at least once in the lifetime by every able-bodied Muslim.

Chapter 5

GULF WAR: OPERATION DESERT STORM

On 2 August 1990, the Iraqi dictator, Saddam Hussain, invaded Kuwait and occupied the tiny city-state within two days. The reasons for the invasion are debated but could be a combination of debt servicing by Iraq, the surge in the oil production levels by Kuwait, or outright territorial ambitions on the part of Iraq. Iraq borrowed from Kuwait a total of US$ 14 billion during eight years of disastrous war with Iran. Kuwait's demands for repayment of the loan and Iraq's inability to repay were met with an increase in Kuwait's oil production levels, which kept Iraq's revenues down, further weakening Iraq's economy. Kuwait kept its oil production levels above the mandatory quota under OPEC during the eighties. Kuwait's refusal to reduce these levels further incensed the Iraqi dictator, who interpreted it as Kuwait's aggression against the Iraqi economy, which precipitated the Iraqi invasion and occupation of Kuwait. The Kuwait-Iraq border dispute involved Iraqi claims to Kuwait territory and was another angle to the conflict. The borders of

Kuwait were demarcated with Iraq by the British in 1922, making Iraq virtually a landlocked country. However, Iraq did not ratify it and continued to claim the Kuwaiti islands of Bubiyan and Wafra.

Iraqi invasion was met with an armed conflict between Iraq and a 42 nations coalition led by the United States. The United States had its reasons for entering into the conflict. The United States disliked the proximity of Iraq to the Soviet Union during the Cold War. The other irritant was the constant outbursts of the Iraqi dictator against the State of Israel, and Saddam was also supporting guerrillas and terrorist groups against Israel. The coalition strategy was divided into two phases: *Operation Desert Shield* from August 1990 to January 1991, and *Operation Desert Storm,* which started the hostilities and aerial bombardment on 17th January 1991 and continued till Kuwait was liberated on 28 February 1991.

Facing defeat in the Gulf War, Saddam Hussein adopted a scorched earth policy. The retreating Iraqis burned more than 600 oil fields in a widespread territory in southern Kuwait. A massive pall of dense black smoke engulfed Kuwait and neighbouring Saudi Arabia for several months. It took eight months to extinguish all the fires.

In July 1990, during the summer vacations of my daughters studying in London, when my wife from Kuwait joined them, I booked my seat on British Airways for London for the morning of Ist August 1990. I arrived in London on the evening of the same day. Saddam invaded Kuwait on the intervening night of August 2nd, 1990. I spent time in London in a rented dinghy room till March 1991, when I was relocated to the medical faculty of Bahrain. The students of the medical faculty of Kuwait, along with their families, fled to safer places in the Gulf countries. They were gathered by the Kuwaiti Government in exile to Bahrain to continue their studies there. Academic staff was needed to supervise their teaching in Bahrain, and that is when I was approached in London to proceed to Bahrain. Soon, I established my residence in Bahrain, where I was with my students. After the liberation of Kuwait, I was asked by the Dean of Kuwait's medical faculty to visit Kuwait and survey the damage caused to the medical faculty. In Kuwait, I saw a black cloud of smoke hanging in the sky with no sunlight filtering in. All the faculty departments were looted of equipment and supplies and vandalized. The residential quarters of the academic staff at the Shuwaikh campus were also ransacked and vandalized. My flat was no exception. When the Kuwait faculty re-opened in September 1991, reconstruction and the furnishing of the departments started. Regular teaching began in November 1991.

The misguided invasion of Kuwait brought disastrous consequences not only for Iraq and the region but also to the person of Saddam and other ruling cliques of the Iraqi Ba'ath party. Iraq had to pay billions of dollars in compensation to the losses caused to Kuwait. More importantly, Iraq was forced to recognize and ratify

Kuwait's sovereignty. The ratification was lodged with the United Nations.

Figure 5.1. Close-up view of Kuwaiti Oil fire (https://commons.wikimedia. org/wiki/File:Kuwaiti_Oil_Well_Fire.jpg) by Wikimedia user 'EdJF'. This image is licensed under CC BY-SA 4.0 (https://creativecommons.org/ licenses/by-sa/4.0/deed.en).

Oil Fires in Kuwait. Oil fields were put on fire by the retreating Iraqi forces. Oil Lakes (image Lower Left) were also burnt. It took eight months to control more than 600 fires.

Chapter 6

SOCIETAL TRANSFORMATION

Before the discovery of oil, Kuwait was a small town with mud-brick-long courtyard houses. The town was devoid of city transport and other modern amenities. The main occupations of the people were pearl diving, fishing, seafaring, boat building, herding, and trade. Kuwait established a maritime port in the latter half of the eighteenth century. It gradually became a commercial centre for transit trade between Iraq, the Arabian Peninsula, Oman, Persia, and India. Kuwait also established a trading route between the Persian Gulf and the Mediterranean port of Aleppo. Kuwait attracted business people from surrounding cities, notably from Basra, Iraq. Kuwaiti high seas sailing vessels, Dhows, were plying in the Arabian Sea and Indian Ocean and soliciting trade from the cities on the west coast of India, notably Cochin, the east coast of Africa, and Singapore. Kuwaiti dhows developed an excellent reputation as a sturdy and secure high-sea vessel. These trade patterns laid the foundation of Kuwait's economy from the 1670s until WWII.

With the discovery of oil in 1938, Kuwaiti society was gradually transformed from a seafaring merchant community to a city-based people developing small commercial establishments. The Iranian business migrants played a significant role in this transformation. Kuwait also established educational and professional institutions to help the country become self-sufficient in the educated cadres. There was a lack of locally qualified people to run these institutions. To overcome this problem, Kuwait developed a two-pronged strategy of allowing qualified and experienced cadres from abroad to come to the country and run these institutions and, secondly, sending the prospective high school leavers abroad, notably England,

Figure 6.1. *Pre-Oil Kuwait City*. Collection of old mud-brick houses of the Kuwaitis. 1920-1930. Courtesy Professor Hussain Dashti.

Figure 6.2. **Left**: Arab Nouveau villa in Kuwait (https://commons. wikimedia.org/wiki/File:Arab_Nouveau_Villa,_Kuwait.jpg) by Dr Basil Al Bayati. This image is dedicated to the public domain under CC0 1.0 (https://creativecommons.org/publicdomain/zero/1.0/?ref=chooser-v1). Right: Hanging Garden's Residence in Kuwait(https://es.wikipedia.org/ wiki/Archivo:Hanging_Garden_Villa,_Kuwait.jpg) by Dr Basil Al Bayati. This image is dedicated to the public domain under CC0 1.0 (https:// creativecommons.org/publicdomain/zero/1.0/?ref=chooser-v1.

to get the required training. Initially, qualified people from Arabic-speaking countries were preferred. The only Arab country that could provide such professionals in large numbers was Egypt. Egyptians started filling administrative and professional positions, mostly at lower levels. The Egyptian administrative structure was an old multi-level accountability bureaucratic system requiring clearance of documents from different offices. Egyptians introduced their administrative model in the country, providing teachers to run the schools of Kuwait and almost wholly controlling the health care in Kuwait. Egyptian doctors, paramedics, and nurses flooded the hospitals.

Egyptian educational, professional, and administrative institutes were working overtime to cope with these demands, not only from Kuwait but also from the Gulf states and other countries in the Middle East. Senior administrative, educational, and professional cadres were either senior qualified Kuwaitis or mostly expatriates from English-speaking countries, South Asian countries, and India. It was virtually the situation when I arrived in Kuwait in 1980.

Six days of war between Israel and the Arab coalition resulted in the victory of Israel and displaced thousands of Palestinian Arabs from their homeland. Kuwait was the first country to allow them visa-free entry, and thousands landed there. In Kuwait, they established their residences in the city's oldest residential area, Hawalli, on the periphery of the city centre. The literacy rate among the Palestinians was very high—almost 96%. They occupied all the available office, administrative, technical, and paramedical positions and positions of school teachers in Kuwait. Palestinians maintained large families, and before the Iraqi invasion of Kuwait, their numbers swelled to almost 400,000. With their educational background and the strength of their numbers, they started demanding political rights reserved for the native Kuwaitis. When Iraq invaded Kuwait, their sympathies lay with Saddam Hussain and not with Kuwait, which offered them succour at the time of their need and provided them with means for survival, jobs, free education, and healthcare. When Kuwait was liberated in 1991, many Palestinians, fearing reprisals from Kuwiaitis, left for Jordan voluntarily. Most of those who remained were asked to leave. Few Palestinians remained in Kuwait after their mass exodus to Jordan. Their current population is estimated at around 40,000. Kuwait also expelled Iraqis and Yemenis after the Gulf War. Around 1,50,000 stateless Beduons were also expelled and settled near the Iraqi border after the war.

Figure 6.3. Images from *Pre-Oil Old* Souk and Business Street of Kuwait in Sharq, Kuwait. Courtesy Professor Hussain Dashti.

As Kuwait grew exponentially on the strength of petro dollars, more and more expatriate labour, workers, professionals, and health-care personnel started coming to Kuwait. The total population of Kuwait in the 2023 census was 4.82 million. Of these, 1.53 million were

Kuwaiti citizens, and the bulk of 3.29 million people were expatriates from almost 100 countries. Kuwaitis constituted 32 % of the population, a minority in their country.

The living standards of the Kuwaitis have significantly improved, and in recent times, Kuwait City has expanded in all directions. It is rare to see poor Kuwaitis; all are middle- and upper-middle-class, and there are many rich and super-rich people. The big business houses are flourishing, and so are the small and middle-level businesses of expatriates.

From 1946 to 1982, the urbanization of Kuwait started in earnest. Decades of urban planning have transformed a once quiet, peaceful, tolerant, and homogeneous society, giving rise to a self-centred, intolerant, and divisive society using its energy and resources to promote itself at the cost of marginalized sections. However, this period also brought material gains for Kuwait and ushered in peace and prosperity more than at any time in its history. Culture and arts were promoted, and the citizens enjoyed a luxurious standard of living. This period has been described as the '*Golden Era of Kuwait.*' In 1952, the country became the largest exporter of oil in the region. With this prosperity, Kuwait developed a liberal outlook and encouraged a more unrestrained press than anywhere in the Gulf. Kuwaiti people enjoyed greater freedom of expression. Literary activity and publication of Arab literature and magazines started.

In June 1961, Kuwait became independent of British control. Amir Abdulah Al-Salem Al-Sabah was installed as the first Amir of independent Kuwait. Kuwait National Day, instead of being celebrated in the heat of June, was moved to 25 February, the date of the coronation of Amir Abdullah. He established the institutions of the State of Kuwait: its first constitution in 1962 and the first Parliament in 1963. Amir Abdullah is regarded as the father of modern Kuwait, and during his rule, Kuwait started to modernize. Around this time, Kuwait was considered the most developed country in the region.

Kuwait was the first in the Gulf region to take steps to emancipate women from being confined to the seclusion of their houses and raising children. Kuwaiti women now actively participate and, at times, excel in all spheres of public life. Co-education at the university level is open to them, and they are training in increasing numbers in professional education and humanities. Kuwaiti women now occupy the positions of doctors, engineers, lawyers, educators, IT professionals, and administrators. They participate in the country's political process and have served as ministers in the government. The Kuwaiti women have come of age.

Kuwait Investment Authority, the world's first sovereign fund, and the Future Generation Fund (FGF) were founded in 1953 to divert the surplus state funds into these investments. These funds came in handy during the Iraqi invasion of Kuwait in 1990. From the 1970s onwards, Kuwait scored the highest in the international rating on the Human Development Index.

Kuwait is one of the wealthiest countries in the world. The Kuwaiti Dinar is the strongest currency in the world. The per capita income of Kuwait is USD 70,000.

Kuwait invested heavily in infrastructure. Modern 6-8 lanes and highways crisscrossed the city. The iconic Gulf Road straddles the coast of Kuwait to the border with Saudi Arabia in the south. The Kuwaiti royal family and citizens used this road to flee to Saudi Arabia to escape Iraqi aggression.

Chapter 7

GOLDEN SANDS OF KUWAIT

Kuwaiti desert is vast, around 18000 square kilometres and desert peoples and animals have trodden upon its brown sands for millennia. These very sands nurtured the desert people destined to live and survive in harsh weather conditions. These sands saw the origin of a unique Arab culture and traditions closely guarded till today.

Like the rest of Arabia, Kuwait has extreme weather conditions, which are very hot in the summer and cooler in the winter. There is little rainfall, particularly during winter months. During summer, hot winds blow from the desert, and when they become turbulent, precipitate sand storms and engulf the city. Desert sand enters the homes, a tacit reminder to the city dwellers that they were once one with these golden sands.

In addition to environmental pollution, these storms jeopardize respiratory health and can precipitate asthmatic attacks and allergies in susceptible individuals. The dust and sand can manifest as full-blown storms or suspended dust storms in the air, causing perpetual breathing problems. They usually occur in the summer months, from May to August. The source of the dust and sand entering Kuwait has been identified to be from the vast Iraqi desert areas between the Tigris and Euphrates rivers 250 km from the Kuwaiti border with Iraq. Recent Meteorological administration reveals that Kuwait gets suspended dust storms and fully blown sand storms around 137 days per year. During these storms, all city life comes to a standstill, with no air, road, or sea traffic, causing financial losses.

Figure 7.1. Golden Sands of the Kuwaiti Desert. A picture was taken in the desert of Kuwait during a sandstorm (https://commons.wikimedia.org/wiki/File:Q8desert.jpg) by Ahmad Al-Shami (Wikimedia user 'Kuwaitsoccer'). This image is licensed under CC BY-SA 3.0 (https://creativecommons.org/licenses/by-sa/3.0/)

Kuwait Bay (Jun al Kuwayt) is the most prominent feature, and it indents the Kuwaiti shoreline by about 40 kilometres. White sandy beaches are spread along the coastline of the Gulf. The entire stretch of the west coast of the Gulf is dotted with white sandy beaches and beachside chalets of the affluent Kuwaitis. These beaches are private, and in between them are the public beaches.

During my extended stay in Kuwait, we frequently visited the chalet of Professor Abdullah Al-Bader, dean of medical faculty and later president of Kuwait University, who has a beautiful stretch of beach with white sands.

Figure 7.2. Chalet of Dr Abdullatif. **Left:** Waters of the Arabian Gulf lashing the Beach. **Right:** Relaxing in the verandah of the Chalet. Dr Abdullatif is facing the camera and wearing a white cap. Also seen is the author in a black cap. Dr Hussain Dashti is next to Dr Abdullatif. Mr Sadiq and Mr Lubomir are also seen next to me. Courtesy Professor Abdullatif Al-Bader.

Figure 7.3. White Sands of Kuwait. Kuwait Beach (https://commons. wikimedia.org/wiki/File:Kuwait_beach.jpg) by Wikimedia user 'Ashashyou.' This image is licensed under CC BY-SA 3.0 (https://creativecommons.org/ licenses/by-sa/3.0.

Figure 7.4. **Left:** Sea City has pioneered many construction challenges and techniques in Kuwait (https://commons.wikimedia.org/wiki/ File:Sabah_Al_Ahmad_Sea_City_-_Phase_4_Lagoon.JPG) by Wikimedia user 'Saasckuwait.' This image is licensed under CC BY-SA 3.0 (https:// creativecommons.org/licenses/by-sa/3.0/). **Right:** Sea City has pioneered many construction challenges and techniques in Kuwait (https://commons. wikimedia.org/wiki/File:Sabah_Al_Ahmad_Sea_City_-_Phase_A3_Aerial_ Shot.JPG) by Wikimedia user 'Saasckuwait.' This image is licensed under CC BY-SA 3.0 (https://creativecommons.org/licenses/by-sa/3.0/).

Figure 7.5. **Left:** Sea City has pioneered many construction challenges and techniques in Kuwait (https://commons.wikimedia.org/wiki/File:Sabah_Al_Ahmad_Sea_City_-_Phase_A2.jpg) by Wikimedia user 'Saasckuwait.' This image is licensed under CC BY-SA 3.0(https://creativecommons.org/licenses/by-sa/3.0/). Right: Sea City has pioneered many construction challenges and techniques in Kuwait (https://commons.wikimedia.org/wiki/File:Sabah_Al_Ahmad_Sea_City_-_Phase_A2_and_Phase_A3.jpg) by Wikimedia user 'Saasckuwait.' This image is licensed under CC BY-SA 3.0 (https://creativecommons.org/licenses/by-sa/3.0/).

Sabah Al-Ahmad Sea City is in the making. The city's development has progressed to Phase 3 out of 10. The upper Right image shows Phase 3 of the project.

Sabah Al-Ahmad Sea City is a remarkable architectural development in the Ahmadi area, south of Kuwait. It is styled after the Al-Jumeirah Beach City of Dubai but on a much broader scale and with a different approach to building it. Unlike Al-Jumeirah, reclaimed sealand was not used; instead, large water channels were dug in the desert land to make artificial islands, waterways, and beaches. Construction of the first phase of the city was started in 2004. Construction of the third phase is in progress. The completion of the remaining phases would take 25 years.

Al Khiran Resort is the oldest resort in Ahmadi, 100 km south of Kuwait City. It was opened in 1987 and became one of Kuwait's popular getaways. It occupies almost 2 km of sandy beaches and seafront, ideal for sailing, boating, and sea sports. The resort has lush green lawns and shopping facilities. Chalets with beautiful Gulf views offer comfort for long-term stays.

Part III

Pearls of Arabian Gulf

Chapter 1

BEAUTIFUL BAHRAIN

The Island of Bahrain is located in a bay on the southwestern coast of the Arabian Gulf. It has been inhabited since ancient times when it was the centre of the Dilmun civilization, a trading community. Because of its strategic location in the Arabian Gulf, it came under the influence of Sumerians, Persians, Babylonians, Portuguese, Arabs, and British. Portuguese ruled the island from 1521 to 1602, and Persians ruled from 1602 to 1783. Ruins of the Portuguese are preserved in the Qal'at l-Bahrain, the ancient seat of the Dilmun civilization. Persian rule brought a significant number of Iranian settlers engaged in fishing activities. Al Khalifah's family from the Al-Hasa province of the Arab Peninsula ruled Bahrain from 1783. The Sheikhs of the family have been rulers of Bahrain ever since. To ward off excursions from Persians, Egyptians, Germans, and Russians, Bahrain signed a treaty with Britain in 1861 and became a British protectorate till 1968, when British influence ceased. Sheikh Issa ibn Salman Al Khalifah proclaimed independence in 1971, and the State of Bahrain was established with Manama as the capital. Recently, Bahrain has been styled as the Kingdom of Bahrain and the King of Bahrain as the head of state.

Figure 1.1. **Upper**: BahrainFort(https://www.flickr.com/photos/40271931@N00/3190456802/) by Flickr user, 'Peter Dowley.' This image is licensed under CC BY 2.0 (https://creativecommons.org/licenses/by/2.0/deed.en **Lower Left**: The Tomb of Yesterday (https://www.flickr.com/photos/21386962@N05/2638378123) by Flickr user 'jdl_deleon.' This image is licensed under CC BY 2.0 (https://creativecommons.org/licenses/by/2.0/deed.en# **Lower Right**: Arad Fort (https://commons.wikimedia.org/wiki/File:AradFort.jpg) by Wikipedia user 'Shijaz Abdulla / Shijaz'. This image is dedicated to the public domain.

Because of its Island status and greater access to sea travel, the people of Bahrain were greatly exposed to outside influences. Bahrain has developed a more tolerant cosmopolitan society than its neighbours, particularly Saudi Arabia. People, particularly from Saudi Arabia, would often travel to Bahrain across the causeway connecting the two countries to spend carefree weekends in Bahrain and enjoy the comforts that otherwise were prohibited in conservative Saudi Arabia. While promoting and protecting its Arab-Islamic heritage, Bahrain was more amenable to modernization and Westernisation than Saudi Arabia.

I arrived in Bahrain in April 1991, immediately after the end of the Gulf War, from London, where I spent my time when the Gulf War started. The President of Kuwait University, a former Dean of the Faculty of Medicine, who was also displaced and living in London, arranged for me to go to Bahrain and supervise the teaching of the displaced Kuwaiti medical students collected at the Bahrain Medical Faculty. I spent six months in Bahrain, which gave me ample time to explore the island and its people.

Figure 1.2. **Left:** Northern Side of the al-Fateh Grand Mosque, Manama, Bahrain (https://commons.wikimedia.org/wiki/File:Manama_alFateh_Grand_Mosque_Exterior_Norden_3.jpg) by Wikimedia user 'Zairon.' This image is licensed under CC BY-SA 4.0 (https://creativecommons.org/licenses/by-sa/4.0/deed.en). **Right:** Saint Christopher's Catedral inManama,Bahrain(https://commons.wikimedia.org/wiki/File:Saint_Christopher%27s_Catedral_Bahrain_A_865.jpg) by Wikimedia user 'Ciacho5'. This image is licensed under CC BY-SA 3.0 (https://creativecommons.org/licenses/by-sa/3.0/deed.en).

Bahraini people are ethnically diverse people. Sunni and Shia Islamic populations are almost evenly distributed in Bahrain. Sometimes, conflicts of interest on religious grounds cause turbulence in otherwise pacific society. Bahrani society is liberal and tolerant. The official religion of Bahrain is Islam, and 74% of the population adheres to it; they permit other religions to operate and build their religious places of worship.

Figure 1.3. **Right:** Inner Courtyard of Sri Krishna Temple at Night, Manama, Bahrain (https://commons.wikimedia.org/wiki/File:Manama_al-Fateh_ Grand_Mosque_Exterior_Norden_3.jpg) by Wikimedia user 'Zairon.' This image is licensed under CC BY-SA 4.0 (https://creativecommons.org/ licenses/by-sa/4.0/deed.en). **Left:** Sikh Gurdwara, Budaiya, Bahrain.From World Gurdwaras. Bahrain.

There are Christian churches, Hindu temples, Sikh Gurdwaras, and a Jewish synagogue(till recently). Working-class people, primarily expatriates, are treated with care, and an environment conducive to optimal performance is provided. Talent is respected, and students at colleges and universities are eager to learn and appreciate their teachers, local or expatriate, in equal measure. They are generally disciplined and do not create problems for themselves or their teachers, institutions, and society. Except for the contact over teaching sessions, there are no other avenues through which teachers and students interact socially. The students generally confine their collective activities among themselves.

Arabian Gulf University College of Medicine and Medical Sciences was established in 1980. Gulf states, including Kuwait, supported it. During the Iraqi invasion of Kuwait in 1990, the dispersed Kuwaiti medical students were collected at this medical college to continue their studies. Some of the academic staff, including myself, were also relocated to Bahrain to supervise the teaching of the Kuwaiti medical students.

Bahrainis uphold their religious occasions and celebrate them passionately. They include three major festivals: Eid al-Fitr, Eid al-Adha, and Prophet Muhamand's birthday. Bahraini Muslims also commemorate *Ashura*. It is celebrated mainly by the Country's Shia Muslims or Ajam (Irani Shia). A small section of Bahrainis profess Christianity and celebrate their religious festivals. About 75% of Bahrain's labour force is from India, mainly Hindu, with some Muslims.

Traditional Bahraini dress conforms to the general Arab dress of the Arabian Peninsula. Thobe or dishdasha is the male dress with conventional headdresses of Kaffiyah, ghutra, and agal or camel hair cord. Bahrani women dress in the traditional Arab dress of abaya, a long, loose-fitting gown worn with the black cloth on the head called the hijab. Western-style clothing is also common in Bahrain. The Bahrani food habits are identical to the general Arab food habits, and the diet is rich in different types of cooked meats and rice. Iranian bread is the staple food. Other typical food includes muhammar, a sweet brown rice with sugar or dates; Shawarmah, a pit-roasted lamb; and chicken or beef preparation. Like other Arab societies, sitting in coffee shops and sipping coffee is a great pastime.

Traditional handicraft industries are popular with Bahrainis. Several types of these industries exist, and artisans chisel out various shapes of metal, wood, cloth, and carpet designs. They sell their wares at small shops in the souks of Manama. There is a small art community, and the Bahrain National Museum displays artworks and other historical and prehistoric collections. Art galleries also display artworks. Few other museums are dedicated to the history of petroleum production, pearl diving, and handicrafts.

Bahrain has a rich folk music culture, and *fidjeri* songs once sung by pearl divers still echo in the streets of Bahrain.

The Island of Al-Muharraq is the northernmost island of the Bahrain archipelago and was the first island to be settled by migrant Arab people, later by the occupiers, Portuguese (1521) and Persians (1602). It came into the control of the Al Khalifah family, who migrated from the Arab Peninsula in 1783 and established a dynasty ruling the island till today. Because of its defensive position, Muharraq was the capital of Bahrain until 1923.

Manama is the modern capital and the largest city in Bahrain. It is an important trading centre in the Arabian Gulf region and has been a centre of major trade routes since antiquity. It is a gateway to the central Bahrain Island. Manama was established in the 1800s and grew gradually under the shadow of Bahrain's twin city of Muharraq, the capital of Bahrain, till 1923. After that, Manama was established as the capital.

Figure 1.4. Bab Al Bahrain, Bahrain (https://commons.wikimedia.org/wiki/File:BabAlBahrain1.jpg) by Wikimedia user 'Mike Odin.' This image is licensed under CC BY-SA 3.0 (https://creativecommons.org/licenses/by-sa/3.0/).

With the discovery of oil, Manama's importance grew, and it started developing as the major financial hub in Bahrain and the Gulf region. In 2012, the Arab League recognized Manama as the capital of Arab Culture and a beta global city by the Globalization and World Cities Research Network.

The city's major attractions are its National Museum and the iconic Bab Al Bahrain in the city centre. This landmark gate of the city opens into the oldest souk, the Souk of Bahrain. The souk is a traditional Arab-style souk known for the spice trade. There is a gold souk within this souk, which offers the most extensive collection of gold jewellery. Manama's city nightlife is glamorous. Its several 4-5-star hotels have colourful nightclubs, and the mujra dance is performed in some of them. Mujra dance is the celebrated dance once cherished by the Mughal Emperors of India. This dance is a major attraction for people from other Gulf countries. During my six-month stay, I enjoyed all that Bahrain had to offer.

The Malaysian island of Penang and the Arab island of Bahrain are strategically located on both countries' maritime trading routes. The Malay people of Penang and the Arab people of Bahrain developed traditionally, such as maritime trading communities, small businesses, and fishing. It was not until the arrival of immigrants that the actual development of both islands started. Penang's development began with the arrival of the British colonizers in the 18th century. Thousands of Chinese from mainland China and some South Indians flooded the Island. They opened small and big businesses, stimulated trading activities, and allowed import and export businesses to flourish. Penang became one of the major trading seaports in the Straits of Malacca. The British also benefitted from these activities, raising several administrative buildings, offices, and residences. Some of these buildings exist today. High-rise residential and commercial buildings appeared as the business activities of the Chinese trading community prospered.

Before the arrival of the British colonizers, Iranian-origin immigrants were already well entrenched in Bahrain's business sector. With the arrival of the British, immigration, mainly from Iran, doubled, and Iranian businesses flourished on the Island. The capital city of Manama developed, and high rises started appearing.

In both islands, the immigrant communities were the backbone of creating wealth. For Penang, it was the resident Chinese and, to some extent, Indians and Malays, whereas in Bahrain, the Iranian business community contributed along with local Arab traders. Arabs have been accomplished traders and have excelled in overseas sailing and trading since ancient times. They invented the ocean-going sturdy dhow, and almost all the Gulf Arab states were skilful in launching it. The business acumen of the Iranian settlers was an added help. It was not the case with Penang. The Indigenous Malays have lived off their lands since ancient times. They did not diversify to any significant extent to venture into business, small or big. The immigrant Chinese were accomplished traders, and their arrival in Penang and mainland Malaysia took the business to new heights, so much so that they controlled all the significant corporate commercial activity. Chinese are the backbone of the Penang and Malaysian economies, owning 60-70% of its share.

These two islands reflect the realities and contrasts between the Malay people of Penang and the Arab people of Bahrain. These two islands contrast the study of two cultures and can be projected to understand the veracities of the peoples of Peninsular Malaya and the Arab Peninsula.

Chapter 2

EXOTIC DUBAI

Dubai's history unfolded when the Bani Yas tribe, headed by Maktoum bin Butli, moved from the Arabian Peninsula and settled in the Shindagha Peninsula at the mouth of Dubai Creek in 1833. Maktoum declared independence from Abu Dhabi and developed the town, known as Al Wasl, as a fishing village. The word Dubai comes from the phrase *dabba,* which means "to creep," referring to the slow flow of the inland Dubai Creek. Muhammad al-Idrisi mapped the coast of UAE in the tenth century and left a written record of the area. Gasparo Balbi, a jeweller in Venice, visited the area in 1580 and left details of the pearling industry of Dubai and other villages that now constitute the UAE.

The Dubai rulers retained their independence by putting the neighbouring sheikhdoms against each other. Since 1835, Dubai has signed various agreements with Britain, finally placing its foreign relations under British control in 1892. When Britain finally left the Persian Gulf in 1971, Dubai became the founding member of the United Arab Emirates.

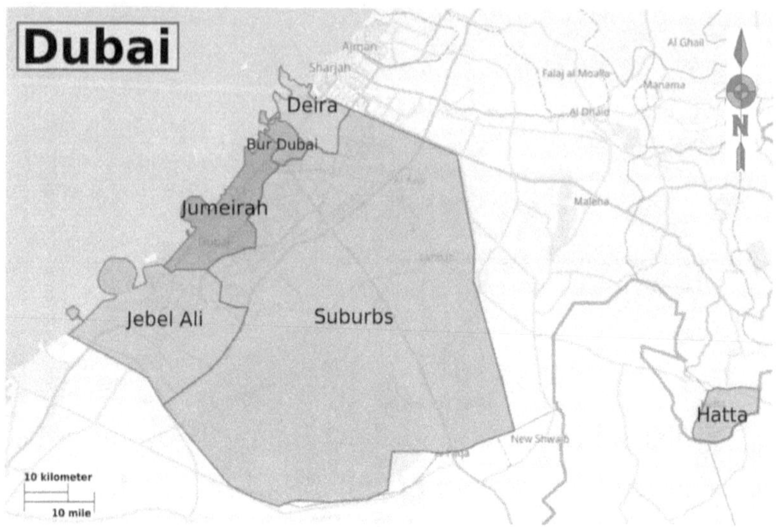

Figure 2.1. Dubainewtravelmap(https://commons.wikimedia.org/wiki/File:Dubai_new_travel_map.png) by Davide Mauro. This image is licensed under CC BY-SA 4.0 (https://creativecommons.org/licenses/by-sa/4.0/deed.en)

The Maktoum Sheikhs of Dubai encouraged trade and commerce. The traditional pearl trading, by the 1930s, was replaced with gold, which encouraged foreign merchants, most of whom were from India, to settle in Dubai. 1901, Dubai was established as a free port with no import and export duties. It enhanced direct and reexported trade and increased the importance of the Dubai port. Steamers from Bombay and Persia started calling at the Dubai port, stimulating trade and making the port a regional trading hub. With the discovery of oil in 1966, Dubai's income increased, and combined with the trading wealth, Dubai became a prosperous state.

A wide range of development and construction plans were designed to promote tourism, transport, and industry.

New deepwater ports and dry docks were established, and industrial units were upgraded. The Jebel Ali port and industrial centre were made a free trade zone, which attracted numerous international companies—with the wealth generated from these endeavours, Dubai started the 21st century with a show of a wide range of transportation and construction projects which eventually changed the skyline of the city with high rises and massive towers of unimaginable proportions. A comparison of the old and new Dubai illustrated here would provide a glimpse of the pinnacle of architectural and recreational marvels already created and others in the pipeline.

Dubai started as a fishing village in the 18th century. It grew as a regional trading hub and, with the discovery of oil, progressed rapidly in the early and late 20th century. By the early 21st century, Dubai had established itself as an international tourist destination offering luxuries and beauty in landscaping and high-rise conglomerates. It is also a major global transport hub for airlines, passengers and cargo.

The ruling Sheikhs in the Arabian Gulf countries are traditionally known as Amirs. Dubai is a part of the United Arab Emirates, a federation of seven Gulf emirates, including Dubai. The people, sometimes known as Emiratis, speak Emirati Arabic. The population of Dubai in 2019 was 3.3 million, and only 15% of the population were UAE (Dubai) nationals. 71% of the Emirate's total population was Asian, chiefly Indians. About 461,000 Westerners reside in the UAE, the majority of

Old Dubai

Figure 2.2. **Upper**: Dubai Museum and Al Fahidi Fort (https://www. flickr.com/photos/kimon/34039548871/) by Flickr user 'Kimon Berlin.' This image is licensed under CC BY-SA 2.0 (https://creativecommons. org/licenses/by-sa/2.0/deed.en). **Lower Left:** Al Bastakiya, Dubai (https:// commons.wikimedia.org/wiki/File:Camello_y_campamento,_Al_ Bastakiya,_Dubai,_2009-11-23,_DD_8878.jpg) by Diego Delso (http:// delso.photo). This image is licensed under CC BY-SA 4.0 (https:// creativecommons.org/licenses/by-sa/4.0/). **Lower Right:** Tourism in Dubai (https://commons.wikimedia.org/wiki/File:The_view_of_Dubai_Creek. jpg) by Wikimedia user 'Phil6007'. This image is licensed under CC BY-SA 4.0 (https://creativecommons.org/licenses/by-sa/4.0/.

The population was made up of UAE (Dubai) nationals. 71% of the Emirate's total population was Asian, chiefly Indians. About 461,000 Westerners reside in the UAE, the majority of whom are British expatriates. A mix of

South Asian languages is spoken, but most Asian people speak Hindi and Urdu.

A significant source of inspiration for the rapid development of Dubai came from the present ruler, Sheikh Mohammed bin Rashid Al Maktoum, ruler of Dubai and Vice-President and Prime Minister of UAE. It is amazing to see how a mud-brick village of the 18th century developed into an astonishing metropolis and a trading and tourist hub in the 20th and 21st centuries, among others boasting the tallest building in the world. Dubai is a major global hub for regional and international trade and shipping. The present leadership played a decisive role in achieving it.

New Dubai

Figure 2.3. **Left:** Dubai Water Canal on the side of BusinessBay (https://commons.wikimedia.org/wiki/File:Dubai_Water_Canal_Business_Bay.jpg) by Wikimedia user 'Iwona Rege.' This image is licensed under CC BY-SA 4.0 (https://creativecommons.org/licenses/by-sa/4.0/). **Right:** Ocean Heights, Dubai Marina, UAE (https://www.flickr.com/photos/66984392@N03/8703344257/) by Flickr user 'Aedas_.' This image is licensed under CC BY-SA 2.0 (https://creativecommons.org/licenses/by-sa/2.0/deed.en).

Dubai city has several architectural marvels, including almost thirty exotic towers. At 828.8 meters, Burj Khalifa is the tallest tower in Dubai and the world. Most other towers are part of the 5-7 star hotels. The other more exotic development is the Palm Jumeirah.

Palm Jumeirah is an artificially created archipelago of islands from reclaimed land from the shore of Jumeirah Beach, Arabian Gulf. It is part of a series of developments called Palm Islands, Palm Jebel Ali, and Palm Deira. It has residential units, hotels, malls, and recreational facilities. The construction was started in 2001. By 2009, 28 hotels had opened on the crescent, and 500 families had settled there. It had a population of 25000 in 2022.

The dress code of Dubai Arabs conforms to the dress code of Peninsula Arabs of *thobe* or *dishdasha*, a loose, long ankle-length dress, the top of which is tailored like a shirt. The headdress is keffiyeh or ghutra, a square or a rectangular white or checkered white and red headscarf held in place by a rope band, usually black, called an agal. Dubai Arab women dress in the traditional Arab dress of abaya, a long, loose-fitting gown worn with the black cloth on the head called the hijab. However, Western-style clothing is also common. Most expatriate communities wear Western-style clothes.

With the building boom of the past two decades, Dubai has become a veritable tourist attraction. Dubai offers leisure and pleasure to suit every taste. The recreational facilities are inviting state-of-the-art architectural edifices, and some are to be found in the high-rise tower hotels. In the city, one can explore the wondrous towers of every shape and size and the remarkable awe-inspiring architecture. The beautiful marinas, sandy beaches, water sports, and water parks offer leisure and pleasure with matching serenity. Dubai's tourist potential has remarkably increased in recent years, and tourists worldwide flock to see the city and relish their piece of cake. Dubai is the 7th most visited city in the world. In 2022, Dubai welcomed 14.36 million tourists. Dubai International Airport became the leading airport worldwide after receiving passenger traffic of 70.47 million in 2014.

Figure 2.4. Grand Mosque of Bur Dubai. Grand Mosque @ Bur Dubai (https://www.flickr.com/photos/o_0/15886036342/) by Guilhem Vellut. This image is licensed under CC BY 2.0 (https://creativecommons.org/licenses/by/2.0/deed.en#).

Islam is the state religion of Dubai and is passionately guarded. However, there is religious freedom in Dubai. Dubai has a large Christian, Hindu, Sikh, Baha'i, and Buddhist community residing in the city, practising their religions in their respective religious places, which they can build and own. There is a small but growing Jewish community.

Dubai Arabs are generally polite, well-mannered, and well-behaved people. They respect talent and learned people. However, there are social norms that a visitor must follow, like visiting all of the Arab Peninsula, other Arab countries, and some Asian countries. Since your left hand is considered dirty, always eat or drink with your right hand. Please do not show the soles of your feet or shoes; it is considered disrespectful. Do not cross the path of an Arab or stare at him when he is praying. Drinking in public is illegal. Dress modestly and do not wear clothes that do not cover the whole body in public. Open display of affection is frowned upon. Sharing a hotel room with an unmarried woman is not permitted. During the fasting month of Ramadan, eating and drinking in public is prohibited.

Dubai has almost a dozen Souks dedicated to various goods and utilities. But the most popular is the Dubai Gold Souk. It is located near the Al Ras Metro Station. It has hundreds of shops and vendors selling premium quality gold jewellery. The Souk is famous with South Asian expatriates who traditionally stock gold as an investment for the future. Tourists from around the world also visit it.

Figure 2.5. **Upper**: Hindu Temple, Dubai (https://commons.wikimedia. org/wiki/File:Hindu_Temple_Dubai.jpg) by S Sathiyaraj (Wikimedia user 'Raj. sathiya'). This image is licensed under CC BY-SA 4.0 (https:// creativecommons.org/licenses/by-sa/4.0/deed.en). **Lower Left:** Gurunanak Darbar Dubai church, Churches Complex, Jebel Ali Village, Dubai, UAE (https://commons.wikimedia.org/wiki/File:Gurunanak_Darbar_Dubai,_ Jebel_Ali_Village.jpg) by Jonathan Bowen. This image is licensed under CC BY-SA 4.0 (https://creativecommons.org/licenses/by-sa/4.). **Lower Right**: Roman Catholic church in Churches Complex, Jebel Ali Village, Dubai, UAE (https://commons.wikimedia.org/wiki/File:Catholic_church_in_ Dubai.jpg) by Wikimedia user 'Nepenthes.' This image is licensed under CC BY-SA 3.0 (https://creativecommons.org/licenses/by-sa/3.0

Figure 2.6. **Upper:** Dubai Miracle Garden (https://commons.wikimedia. org/wiki/File:Miracle_Garden_1.jpg) by Wikimedia user 'Dayneferrera.' This image is licensed under CC BY-SA 4.0 (https://creativecommons.org/ licenses/by-sa/4.0/deed.en). **Lower Left:** Dubai Miracle Garden (https:// commons.wikimedia.org/wiki/File:Dubai_Miracle_Garden-Dubai_UAE-Andres_Larin.jpg) by Wikimedia user 'Saaremees.' This image is licensed under CC BY-SA 4.0 (https://creativecommons.org/licenses/by-sa/4.0/deed. en). **Lower Right:** Dubai Miracle Garden (https://commons.wikimedia.org/ wiki/File:Miracle_Garden.jpg) by Wikimedia user 'Sanciacf.' This image is licensed under CC BY-SA 4.0 (https://creativecommons.org/licenses/by-sa/4.0/deed.en).

Figure 2.7. **Upper:** Dubai Miracle Garden (https://commons.wikimedia. org/wiki/File:VAE-dubai-miracle-06.jpg) by Wikimedia user 'Balou46'. This image is licensed under CC BY-SA 4.0 (https://creativecommons. org/licenses/by-sa/4.0/deed.en). **Lower:** Butterfly Garden Dubai (https:// commons.wikimedia.org/wiki/File:VAE-dubai-butterfl-01.jpg) by Wikimedia user 'Balou46'. This image is licensed under CC BY-SA 4.0 (https:// creativecommons.org/licenses/by-sa/4.0/deed.en)

Dubai Miracle Garden is another singular attraction that Dubai offers to tourists. It is the world's most extensive natural flower garden, featuring over fifty million flowers and 250 million plants. The garden is spread over 72000 square meters in the district of Dubailand, launched in 2013. The garden has achieved three Guinness World Records.

Dubai may be considered a 'stand-alone city.' No other place in the Gulf or Arabian Peninsula can match the level of development experienced by this city. In a few years, the city has been transformed to rise to new heights from a sleepy town of brick plaster houses of yesteryears. The tall towers of Dubai reflect the unflinching will and determination of Dubai Sheikhs to launch it as a central international tourist hub backed by petro-dollars. The wisdom of the leaders of yesteryears is paying dividends today. However, Dubai is not reflecting the actual realities of the Arab world at large. It is a city unto itself. It showcases the architectural marvels of beauty and imagination, which even the Guinness Book Of Records was tempted to enlist not once but thrice. Dubai is the pearl of the gulf and a pinnacle of Arab accomplishment.

Bahrain reflects the realities of the Arab world more soberly, as does the island of Penang, which reflects the realities of Peninsular Malaya.

Chapter 3

SERENE MUSCAT

Muscat town is the capital of Oman and is located on the coast of the Gulf of Oman. It is situated on a bay and is surrounded by volcanic mountains. Various indigenous tribes and foreign powers ruled it. Persians, Portuguese, and Ottomans gained city control at different historical points. Portuguese gained control of Muscat and the adjacent coast in 1508. They maintained a trading post and a naval base. Two 16th-century Portuguese forts overlook the town.

Muscat was an important port town in the Gulf of Oman and attracted foreign traders and settlers, including Persian, Baloch, and Sindhis. During the rule of Sultan Qaboos bin Said, the city progressed rapidly with infrastructure development and a vibrant economy. It developed into a multi-cultural and multi-ethnic society. Muscat is termed a Beta-Global City by the Globalisation and World Cities Network.

Old Muscat

Figure 3.1. Old Muscat. **Upper Left:** Old Muscat (https://commons. wikimedia.org/wiki/File:Old_Muscat.jpg) by Wikimedia user 'Mai-Sachme.' This image is licensed under CC BY-SA 3.0 (https://creativecommons. org/licenses/by-sa/3.0/). **Upper Right:** Inside of Harbour of Maskat with Castle at Entrance (https://archive.org/details/bub_gb_6i4wAAAAYAAJ/ page/744/mode/2up?view=theater) from the book 'Explorations in Bible Lands During the 19th Century' by Hermann Vollrat Hilprecht, Immanuel Benzinger, Fritz Hommel, Peter Jensen and Georg Steindorff. This image is in the public domain. **Lower Left:** The city of Muscat, wood engraving of "The thrones and palaces of Babylon and Nineveh" p. 33 (https://commons. wikimedia.org/wiki/File:City_of_Muscat_in_1876.jpg) by John Philip Newman. This image is in the public domain. **Lower Right:** Old Masqat (https://commons.wikimedia.org/wiki/File:Old_Masqat.jpg) by Wikimedia user 'Imbâbah22'. This image is licensed under CC BY-SA 3.0 (https:// creativecommons.org/licenses/by-sa/3.0.

The old city of Muscat is separated from the Modern Muscat by coastal mountains. It is located along the Muttrah Corniche coastal road. The town was built in

1625 and is surrounded by a protective wall with towers. The town's architecture was influenced by Portuguese, Persian, Indian, African, and modern Western influences. The sultan's Indian-style palace was built facing the sea. The National Museum is also located here.

Figure 3.2. A view of Muscat in 1902. A picturesque view of Maskat, "The Persian problem; an examination of the rival positions of Russia and Great Britain in Persia, with some account of the Persian gulf and the Bagdad railway" p. 36 (https://archive.org/details/persianprobleme00whig/page/n35/mode/1up?view=theater) by Whigham, Henry James. This image is in the public domain.

The Al Jalali and Al Mirani forts, built by the Portuguese in the early 16th century, are preserved in good condition. In addition, Muscat has two more forts: Bait Al Maqham and Muttrah Forts. Commercial activity is located in Muttrah, west of Muscat. Muttrah Port is the principal port of Muscat, and Muttrah Souk is the main commercial hub.

More than half of the Omani population is Arab. There is a large concentration of ethnic Balochi who migrated from Balochistan (Pakistan) and Persia. They lived in Oman for centuries but kept their culture and traditions intact. I visited Muscat and Oman a few times and had no problem conversing in Urdu with Balochi Omanis. Omanis are coming out of their tribal heritage and getting modernized. It is a predominately Ibadi Muslim population and observes social customs, though still conservative, less so than neighbouring Saudi Arabia. Women enjoy more freedom in Oman than in other societies of the Peninsula.

Modern View of Old Muscat

Figure 3.3. **Upper Left:** Sultan Qaboos Street in Muscat, Oman (https://commons.wikimedia.org/wiki/File:Sultan_Qaboos_Street_in_ Muscat_2019-11-30.jpg) by Alexey Komarov. This image is licensed under CC BY-SA 4.0 (https://creativecommons.org/licenses/by-sa/4.0/deed.en. **Upper Right:** Riyam Park with incense burner Mabkhara (https://www. flickr.com/photos/143134673@N07/47954080007/) by Eduard Marmet. This image is licensed under CC BY-SA 2.0 (https://creativecommons. org/licenses/by-sa/2.0/deed.en). **Lower Left:** Muttrah, Muscat, and the port. Photo from above the fish market (http://www.ianandwendy.com/ oman/Muscat%20Mutrah/slideshow.htm#17) by Ian Sewell (Wikimedia user 'Isewell'). This image is licensed under CC BY-SA 3.0 (https:// creativecommons.org/licenses/by-sa/3.0. **Lower Right:** Al Alam Palace (https://www.flickr.com/photos/kewl/) by Tristan Schmurr. This image is licensed under CC BY 2.0 (https://creativecommons.org/licenses/by/2.0/ deed.en#).

Figure 3.4. **Left:** Qasr Al Alam Royal Palace in Muscat (Oman) (https://commons.wikimedia.org/wiki/File:Qasr_Al_Alam_Royal_Palace_(4).JPG) by Wikimedia user 'Ji-Elle.' This image is licensed under CC BY-SA 3.0 (https://creativecommons.org/licenses/by-sa/3.0/). **Right:** Supreme Court Of Oman, Muscat, Oman (https://commons.wikimedia.org/wiki/File:001026-Muscat-IMG_6141-2.jpg) by Safa Daneshvar. This image is licensed under CC BY-SA 4.0 (https://creativecommons.org/licenses/by-sa/4.0/deed.en).

In sharp contrast to Dubai, Muscat City is a quiet, peaceful city devoid of the hustle and bustle of a large city. The city's low-rise, mostly white-painted buildings stand in harmony with nature, unlike Dubai, a spoiled rich town with buildings and tower after tower trying to reach the paradise of heavens and challenging the nature of their prowess. Muscat's serenity and simplicity are more inviting than the bewilderment of a mega city next door. The comparison of Old Muscat with New Muscat is just academic. The architecture is still the same, though much more refined in New Muscat, while the modesty of architecture and simplicity of buildings are retained. It is not a New Muscat but a Modern View of Old Muscat. Figure 3.2, images 'Lower Left' and 'Lower Right' amply explain it.

Omanis wear traditional Arab dress, which is common among the Peninsula Arabs. Most Omani men wear dishdasha, and the distinctive male headgear consists of a light turban of cotton or wool cloth called *muzzar*. However, younger people prefer to wear a rounded Omani cap or *Kuma*. The cap is considered their national heritage, though it is believed to have originated in Zanzibar, a former colony of Oman. Many men carry a curved dagger called *Khanjar* tucked in their waistbands. Omani women wear brightly coloured clothes and jewellery. The traditional dress consists of a loose gown over loose-fitting slacks or sirwal. A long flowing scarf covers the head.

Figure 3.5. Omani Cap or Kuma. Omanis (Arabic: الشعب العماني) are the nationals of Oman (https://commons.wikimedia.org/wiki/File:Omanis_14_ن ا عـمـ م_درم.jpg) by Mostafa Meraji. This image is licensed under CC BY-SA 4.0 (https://creativecommons.org/licenses/by-.

Most Omani social gatherings happen during mealtime. A typical meal includes rice, spiced lamb or fish, dates, and coffee or tea. Incense or frankincense, produced in Oman, is burned at the end of the meal.

Omani, like the rest of the Arab and Islamic world, observe the standard Islamic holidays of Eid al-Fitr and Eid al-Adha, as well as the birthday of the Prophet. Other occasions celebrated are National Day (commemorating the expulsion of the Portuguese in the 17th century) and the birthday of the reigning sultan. Omanis are liberal in their religious outlook and permit other religions to observe their religious occasions and build their places of worship. There are Hindu temples, Sikh Gurdwaras, and Christian churches in Oman.

Figure 3.6. Muscat (https://commons.wikimedia.org/wiki/File:Shiva_temple,_Muscat.jpg) by **Left:** Shiva temple Wikimedia user 'Banksboomer.' This image is licensed under CC BY-SA 4.0 (https://creativecommons.org/licenses/by-sa/4.0/deed.en). **Right:** Church of the Holy Sepulchre, Golgotha (Calvary) (https://www.flickr.com/photos/16185355@N00/1800593205) by Maxim Massalitin. This image is licensed under CC BY-SA 2.0 (https://creativecommons.org/licenses/by-sa/2.0/deed.en).

Several museums in Muscat and the rest of Oman preserve the country's culture and history. The museums include the Oman Museum, located outside Muscat, established in 1974, the National Museum, the Natural History Museum, and others. The Royal Omani Symphony Orchestra in Muscat was founded in the 1980s. During one of my visits to Oman, I attended an opera performance.

Oman's music is traditional Arab folk music sustained by oral transmission from one generation to another. Desert songs praise the robustness of the camel. Al-taghrud is sung as a group song while riding on camels. The Bedouin song Al-Tariq is sung in the same way. These songs retain their original character from place to place in the country. Oman has a long tradition of building ocean-going dhows. Omani sailors and maritime communities have evolved their style of music sung on the high seas while sailing on their dhows. Also, its interaction with coastal people from other countries, such as Egypt, Tanzania, and other places, has enriched Omani music.

The main traditional Omani dances are Alazi, Alayalah, and Taghrodah. Alazi is a sword dance performed by a solo dancer encircled by a group of dancers with swords and rifles. It is usually performed at weddings. Men arranged in two rows perform the Alayalah dance, which is performed in public. Taghrodah is a camel rider's dance without musical instruments.

Part IV

Malaysia and Kuwait

TALE OF TWO PENINSULA

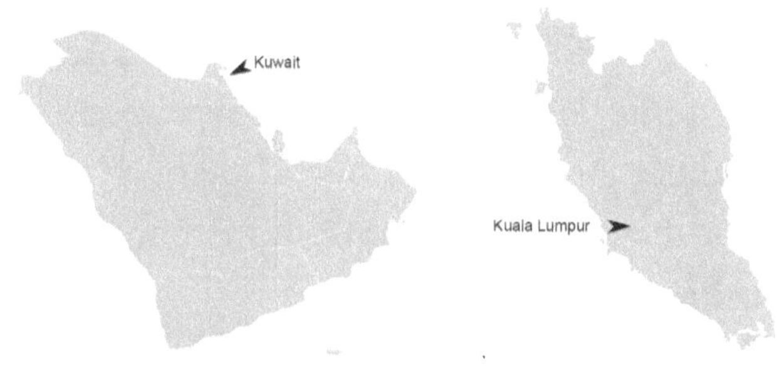

Arabian Peninsula (left, Malay Peninsula (right)
Map not to scale

Malaysian peninsula and Kuwait, located at the northern tip of the Arabian peninsula, are rich countries with many natural resources and a high standard of living. Though miles apart, they share a common religious heritage, Islam, but with different ethnic people, cultures, and traditions. Through Islamic influences, the Malay language is enriched with Arabic words. Still, the basic structure of the language, derived from Malay traditions enriched by the Sanskrit during ancient Indian influences and as a Hindu kingdom till the 15th century, remained virtually intact. However,

Islamic culture and traditions were absorbed into Malay society after the arrival of Islam in Malaysia. Muslim culture is to be viewed in a religious context. Some of the Islamic traditions were Malaynised. The Muslim festival of Eid-ul-Fitr is called Hari Raya Puasa or Hari Raya Aidulfitri, and Eid-ul-Adha is called Hari Raya Haji or Hari Raya Korban. People-to-people contacts are not common, and the only time a small section of Malay people meet with their religious brothers is during Haj, the annual pilgrimage to the holy places of Mecca and Medina. When Arab people from Saudi Arabia visit Malaysia, some local Malay people receive them with great humility and bow in front of them as a mark of respect for the people coming from the holy land where once the Prophet walked.

Culturally, both people are distinctly apart. Malay culture carries the ancient imprints of Indian civilization and local Malay traditions. Islamic traditions enriched the Malay culture and language. It was further influenced by the settlement of Chinese and Indian immigrants during modern times. English influences also affected the culture during British colonial rule. Malaysia is a cultural cauldron where people of many cultures have lived and interacted side by side for centuries. This symbiosis evolved the composite Malay culture which we see and study today.

No significant outside cultural influences affected the peninsular Arabs. They remained independent throughout their history except during a distant Ottoman rule when cultural influences of the Turkish people did not penetrate their society. There were no people-to-people contacts of any significance. Arabic people developed independently and evolved a distinct Arabic civilization and culture influenced by the religion of the Prophet. Islamic faith and Islamic culture developed based on the teachings and writings of the Prophet. Moreover, they exported Arabic Islamic culture to other Islamic societies, including Malaysia.

Both countries are blessed with abundant natural resources, the mainstay of their economies. Saudi Arabia is the largest oil producer and exporter in the world. Muslim world owes about 75% of total world oil reserves. Saudi Arabia tops the Muslim world with 18% of these oil reserves. The remaining oil reserves are distributed among the six other Muslim countries. Figures for Kuwait are 6%, almost the same as the UAE. Kuwait is the most prosperous country, and its Dinar is the highest-valued currency in the world.

Malaysia has a robust economy compared to other Southeast Asian nations. The main contributors are tin, rubber, timber, oil, and manufactured goods. However, on economic grounds, there is no comparison between Kuwait and Malaysia, although Malaysia has been rated the richest among the Southeast Asian countries. I left India in the late sixties of the last century to take up an academic position with the University of Malaya. The country provided Asian life with the Western comforts of those days. I could live comfortably, raise my family, and enjoy modern amenities, but I would hardly have any savings for investments in the future. It was a great concern that made me leave Kuala Lumpur and come to Kuwait.

At the beginning of the eighties of last century, Kuwait was a comfortable modern oil-producing and exporting city. The city and residences were airconditioned to ward off the intense heat of the long summers. The city was built virtually on sands with brown brick-fronted buildings in harmony with the brown sands of the surrounding desert. There was little rainfall. It was a big contrast from Malaysia, a lush green country with tertiary jungles and plenty of rainfall. Kuala Lumpur was warm and humid, and daytime temperatures rarely increased to more than 35C, with much cooler nights. Mosquitos were a perpetual menace. Kuwait had little rainfall, and temperatures in the peak summer months sometimes rose to 50 C and even more, but it was a dry heat. Coming, as it was, from the beautiful, lush green city of Kuala Lumpur and landing in the brown neighbourhoods of the desert sands of Kuwait was initially quite discomforting. But with gradual adaptation to the new environment and other than being absorbed in academic pursuits, the Arab people, their culture, their heritage, and the vast sandy desert and its nomadic tribes offered new horizons to explore, more than adequately compensated for the missing green lands of Malaysia.

In those days, Kuwait began displaying its petrodollars and building its reputation as a rich country. However, little was known about Kuwait and its people in Kuala Lumpur. Most people were ignorant about Kuwait. My school-going daughters studied at a British medium primary school in Kuala Lumpur. One day, I approached the school's headmistress and told her I would soon relocate to Kuwait. She was surprised and said that Kuwait in Arabia is not the place for your daughters and that I would worry about their safety and security. This was the level of ignorance about Arabia and Kuwait from a British school teacher in Kuala Lumpur. When I went to collect air tickets for my and my family's travel from the local travel agent, his counterpart in Kuwait sent with the tickets photos of Kuwait City and its establishments. These photos were shown to the sceptics and the school teacher; they were pleasantly surprised to see Kuwait City's level of civilization and development.

Kuala Lumpur is a multicultural city with a rich composite culture and Malay heritage. On the other hand, Kuwait was guarding its Arabic culture and traditions and, more importantly, its religious legacy. Kuwait did not have the experience of a multicultural society like Kuala Lumpur, and its culture and traditions were inbred. Even if there were a multicultural Kuwaiti society, it was unlikely that it would change the age-old traditions that were the core of its existence. The same holds for the Arabian peninsula and its people.

Recently, Malaysia has been more inclined to adopt, integrate, and create more space for Islamic culture and traditions. It was based on politico-religious compulsions. Establishing a fully evolved Islamic society may have limitations in a multicultural country. Protecting the legitimate interests of other cultures was imperative. Kuwait did not have such compulsions. However, the religious dichotomy has been the cause of some concern. Saudi Arabia established Sunni Islamic religious traditions and supported them in other Islamic societies, including Kuwait. The ancestors of Kuwait brought Sunni Islam to Kuwait. However, there is a section of immigrant society in Kuwait that are the followers of Shia Islamic traditions, which are dominant in Iran. There is sometimes a conflict of interest between the two sections of Islamic society.

Malay Muslims follow the fundamental principles of the Shafi'i school of Sunni Islam. Malays strictly observe the five pillars of Islam: shahada (declaration of faith), prayers, fasting, distribution of alms, and pilgrimage to Mecca for able-bodied Muslims who can afford it. However, some of the fundamental tenets of Islam have been subject to local interpretations. It signifies a dynamic interaction between Islam and Malay culture. Malaysian Islamic society is more or less homogeneous, and the government does not encourage any dichotomy in Malay Islamic society.

I lived in Kuala Lumpur for 12 years and spent almost 30 years in Kuwait. Notwithstanding the ethnic and cultural differences between the two diverse societies separated by hundreds of kilometres, I enjoyed what these two societies had to offer and made the best of my stay. In Malaysia, I absorbed the cultural peculiarities of the multicultural society and adapted to it as much as possible. Since the medium of instruction was English and English became the common written and spoken language of communication with the Malays and other ethnic communities, learning the Malay language was handicapped. Still, I picked up a half-broken Malay to communicate with locals. People-to-people contacts were developed, and it was interesting to study the Malay culture, their style of living, their eating and food habits, their concepts of life and death, and their attitude to life in general. There was an added opportunity in Malaysia to study the culture of the immigrant Chinese community, their outlook on life, their business and money-making expertise, their social and cultural traditions, and exclusiveness. It was also interesting to socialize with Tamil Indian Malaysians and to learn from their ancient culture. Tamil Hindu influence prevailed in Malaya till the 15th century when the Malacca sultanate was established with the conversion of the Malay Hindu Raja Permaisura to Islam after he married a Muslim Indonesian princess renamed Raja Permaisuri Agong or the supreme queen. All Malaysian Queens who followed are styled as such till today. This name carries forward the legacy of the conversion to Islam of Hindu Raja Permaisura and the ushering of Islam in Malaya through his Muslim queen.

With that, the Islamization of Malaya started. Over the centuries of exposure to Tamil Hindu culture, the Malay language was Sanskritized, and Indian customs and traditions were absorbed into Malay society. The names Permaisura and Permaisuri are Sanskrit names. With the introduction of Islam, the Malay language was enriched with Arabic words and religious traditions, but the basic character of the language remained more or less intact.

South Indian Tamils are known for their dance and music styles, which they have perfected over the centuries. The national dance of India, Bharatanatyam, is based on Tamil dance and music traditions. Tamils introduced their culture to Malaysia, and their dances were very popular. Some of the Malay dances have imprints of Tamil music and dance. My wife was very impressed by their dances and wanted our two daughters to learn the Tamil classical dances. A special Tamil music teacher was hired to teach them.

Kuwait's culture and Islamic traditions follow in tandem with the other three prominent countries of the Arabian Gulf, Bahrain, Dubai, and Muscat in Oman. All the Gulf countries draw religious and cultural inspiration from Saudi Arabia. Though Saudi Arabia is still a conservative society, the Gulf countries have evolved to various degrees of social and cultural liberalization. Bahrain is perhaps the most liberal of all the Gulf Arab societies. Nevertheless, all the Gulf countries retain their ethnic and religious structure as guided by Islam.

Kuwait had much to offer for a first-time resident expatriate like me. There was much to learn from the Arabic Kuwaiti culture, the city institutions, and the vast sandy desert, which had much to offer. I explored much of it during my extended stay in Kuwait.

Throughout more than five decades of my professional journey, destiny graciously guided me to traverse the landscapes of two distinct Peninsulas. These geographical realms were separated by physical distance, language nuances, and cultural intricacies. However, amidst these disparities, a unifying thread for these two nations was the reverence for the same religion.

Reflecting on these years, I can unequivocally declare them to be the pinnacle of my existence. They were not merely a period of time spent in academic pursuits but rather an odyssey of exploration and discovery. Each day brought forth new encounters, insights, and perspectives, enriching my life's tapestry with vibrant hues of diversity.

In the words of the eminent Yo-Yo Ma, "I've always felt that my life and my music are interchangeable. I don't feel I have a job. I feel I have a calling. I will never forget that." These sentiments resonate deeply within me, encapsulating the profound connection between vocation and fulfilment. Like Yo-Yo Ma, I, too, have been blessed to embrace my calling wholeheartedly, allowing it to shape my career and very essence.

Indeed, every moment spent within the embrace of these Peninsulas was imbued with a sense of purpose and joy. Each interaction, whether with the students, people, landscapes, or customs, contributed to the mosaic of my experiences, fostering a profound appreciation for the beauty of tapestry thus blended. And so, as I reflect upon these cherished memories, I am filled with gratitude for the opportunity to have lived and worked within the nexus of these rich cultural diversities.

The following lines sum up the crux of the story of this book:

"We must learn about our cultures to understand, in order to love and in order to preserve our common world heritage."

"The Pathway to a Better World Begins with Culture."

Yo-Yo Ma, White House Conference on Culture and Diplomacy.

REFERENCES

PART-1

Chapter 1

1. Peninsular Malaysia. Travelfish.2022.
2. Siddique,Sharon (1961). Some Aspects of Malay-Muslim Ethnicity in Peninsular Malaysia. Contemporary Southeast Asia. 3(1):76-87.
3. Indonesia- The Malay Kingdom of Srivijaya-Palembang. Encyclopedia Britannica, 2019.
4. Wilkinson, R J (1935). Early Indian Influence in Malaysia. Journal of the Malayan Branch of the Royal Asiatic Society. 13(2): 1-16.
5. Bellina, Berenice (2014). "Southeast Asia and the Early Maritime Silk Road." In Guy, John (ed).Lost Kingdoms of Early Southeast Asia: Hindu-Budhist Sculpture 5th to 8th century. Yale University Press. ISBN 978-1-58839524-5.
6. Patricia Ann Matusky, Sooi Beng Tan ed (2004). The Music of Malaysia: The Classical, Folk and Syncretic Traditions. Ashgate Publishing Limited, pp6-7. ISBN 978-0754608318.
7. Braddell, Roland (1937)." An Introduction to the Study of Ancient Times in the Malay Peninsula and the Straits of Malacca. Journal of the Malayan Branch of the Royal Asiatic Society. 15(3): 64-126.
8. Ishtiac Ahmed (2011). The Politics of Religion in South and Southeast Asia. Taylor and Francis. pp129. ISBN 978-1-136-72703-0.
9. Othman, Mohammad Redzuan (2006). The Arab Migration and its Importance in the Historica Development of the

Late Nineteenth and Early Twentieth Century Malaya. World History Association Annual International Conference, California State University, Los Angeles, California.

10. Latifah, Abdul Latiff (2014). The Hadhrami Arabs in Malaya before the Second World War. ResearchGate, vol 23 no. 1.1. DOI 10.22452/sejarah.

11. Juan L. Rodrigues-Flores, Khalid Fakhro, Francisco Agosto-Perez et al. (2016). Indigenous Arabs and descendants of the earliest split from ancient Eurasian populations. Genome Res. 26(2): 151-162.

Chapter 2

1. Pham, Charlotte Min-Ha L. (2012). "Unit 14. Asian Shipbuilding (Training Manuel for the UNESCO Foundation Course on the Protection and Management of the Underwater Cultural Heritage)." Bangkok: UNESCO Bangkok, Asia and Pacific Regional Bureau for Education. ISBN 978-92-9223-414-0.

2. Andaya, Barbara Watson (1982). History of Malaysia. Macmillan International Higher Education. ISBN 978-1-349-16927-6.

3. Zepp, Raymond (1989). "The Chinese in Sarawak." Bulletin De Sinologie Nouville Serie (53):19-21. JSTOR 43436606.

4. Wong, Danny Tze-Ken(1998). The Transformation of an Immigrant Society. A Study of the Chinese in Sabah. Asean Academic. ISBN 78-1-901919-16-5.

5. Kam, Hing Lee; Chee Beng (2000). The Chinese in Malaysia. Oxford University Press. ISBN 978-983-56-0056-2.

6. Niew,Shong Tong (1969). "The Population Geography of the Chinese Communities in Malaysia, Singapore and Brunei." (PDF). The University of London.

7. Swettenham,Frank (1905). "The Straits Settlements and Beyond." The Emire and the Century. London. John Murray. Pp827-834.

8. Min, Yap Kean (2006). Tin mining in Malaysia- Is there any Revival? UniMAP Library Digital Repository. http://dspace.unimap.edu.my.

9. Yap, Suanne (2013). The story of Kiasu: expressions of identity and status via conspicuous consumption: an ethnographic study Singaporean young women in a newly adopted culture. (Masters Thesis). Western Sydney University.

10. Iim, Lisa (2016). "Where the word Kiasu came from and how it spread." South China Morning Post.

11. Ho, Janice T S; Ang C E; Loh. Joanne; Ng, Irene (1998). A preliminary study of Kiasu behavior-Is it unique to Singapore? Journal of Managerial Psychology 13(5/6):359-370.

12. Viswanathan Selvaratnam (1 May 2021)."From Servitude to Underclass: The Empire's South Indian 'Coolies' in Postcolonial Malaysia. *Economic and Political Weekly.* **56** (18). The ancestral root of about 80% of Malaysian Indians is in the British Empire's Madras Presidency (now Tamil Nadu, Telangana, Andhra Pradesh, and Kerala).

13. Saari M Yusof; Dietzenbacher,Eric; Los,Bart (2015). "Sources of Income Growth and Inequality Across Ethnic Groups in Malaysia." 1970-2000. (PDF). World Development.76:311-328.

14. Wang Kefeng 9/1985). The History of Chinese Dance. China Books and Periodicals. Pp25-27. ISBN 978-0835111867.

15. Dragon Dance. Cultural China.com

16. Kernial Singh Sandhu. (1969).Indians in Malaya.Aspects of their migration and settlement (1786-1957). Cambridge, UK. C Cambridge University Press.ISBN 978-0521148139.

17. Northrup, David (1995). Indentured Labour in the Age of Imperialism,1834-1922. Cambridge UK. Cambridge University Press.

18. Breman,Ian 91989). Taming the Coolie Beast: Plantation Society and the Cultural Order in Southeast Asia. New Delhi. Oxford University Press.

19. Agriculture-Malaysia export crops, farming sector. Nationsencyclopedia.com

20. Plantation and Rubber industries of Malaysia. Malaysia Economics Essay. www.uniassigment.com

21. Bhai Maharaj Singh is a freedom fighter of Punjab. (2019). Sikh Research Institute.

22. Kahlon,Swarn Singh Virk, Dr. Hardev Singh (ed). Sikhs in the Asia Pacific. Travelsamong the Sikh Diaspora from Yangon to Delhi.Kobe. New Delhi. Manohar Publishers, New Delhi.

23. "Gobind Singh Deo is Malaysia's first Sikh minister." The Economic Times.

24. "On the Gurdwara Trail in Malaysia". A Spiritual Experience. Sikh Net

25. Malaysia-Religion. Asian Studies: Windows on Asia. Michigan State University.2011.

26. Schiffman, Harold (1998)." Malaysian Tamils and Tamil Linguistic Culture. University of Pennsylvania.

Chapter 3

1. Race War in Malaysia. Time. May 23, 1969.

2. Donald L Horowitz (2003). The Deadly Ethnic Riot. University of California Press. ISBN 978-0-520-23642-4.

3. Slimming John (1969). The Death of a Democracy. John Murray Publishers Ltd. ISBN 978-0-7195-2045-7.

4. Boon Kheng Cheah (2002). Malaysia: The Making of the Nation. Institute of Southeast Asian Studies. ISBN 978-9812301543.

5. Ravallion,Martin 92020). Ethnic Inequality and Poverty in Malaysia. Part I: Inequality. World Development. 134:105040.

6. Durrishah Idris (2003).New Economic Policy and Birth of Malaysia's Own Industrial Relations System. Jurnal Kemanusiaan. ISBN 1675-1930.

7. Musa, M. Bakri (1999). The Malay Dilemma Revisited. Merantau Publishers. ISBN 1-58348-367-5.

8. Ye, Lin-Sheng (2003). The Chinese Dilemma. East West Publishing. ISBN 0-975-1646-1-9.

9. Chinese Community in Malaysia. My China Roots. http://www.mychinaroots.com

10. Cheah, Boon Kheng (2002)." The Tunku as "Founding Father of the Nation." Malaysia: The Making of a Nation. Singapore Institute of Southeast Asian Studies. Pp109-110. ISBN 9812301542.

11. Gayl D.Ness(May 1972). "May 13:Before and After.by Tunku Abdul Raham: Death of a Democracy. By John Slimming: The May 13 Tragedy; A Report by The National Operations Council: The May 13 Incedent and Democracy in Malaysia. by Goh Cheng Tiek.The Journal of Asian Studies. 3193):734-736. JSTOR 2052316.

12. The National Operations Council (1969). The May 13 Tragedy. A report.

13. von Vorys,Karl(1975). Democracy Without Consensus: Communalism and Political Stability in Malaysia. Princeton University Press. ISBN 978-0-691-07571-6.

Chapter 4

1. University of Malaya- The Oldest University in Malaysia. Malaysia Central,2008.

2. Chung Tat, Lim(2013). University of Malaya 1949-1985.Its Establishment, Growth and Development. Kuala Lumpur. University of Malaya Press. ISBN 978-983-100-580-4.

2. Lim, Victor K E (2009). "Medical Education in Malaysia." Medical Teacher. 30(2). 119-123.

3. "Welcome to FACULTY OF MEDICINE." medicine um edu my. 2020.

4. Danaraj, T J (1975). The Report of Establishment and Progress of the Faculty of Medicine, University of Malaya, Kuala Lumpur. Central Printing Unit, Faculty of Medicine, University of Malaya.

5. "Official Portail University of Malaya Medical Centre. ummc edu my,2016.

Chapter 5

1. Malaysia Culture, Cuisine, Traditions. Britannica. Britannica.com

2. Chinese New Year. History.com

3. The Lunar New Year: Rituals and Legends. Asia for Educators. Columbia University.http://afe.easia.columbia.edu

4. Chinese Festivals. Schumm, New York,1952.

5. Chinese Traditional Festivals. New York Press, Beijing.

6. Mead, Jean (2008). How and Why do Indians Celebrate Divalli. Evans Brothers. ISBN 978-0-237-53412-7.

7. Vasudha Narayanan; Deborah Heiligman (2008). Celebrate Diwali. National Geographic Society. ISBN 978-1-4263-0291-6.

8. SuzanneBarchers (2013). The Big Book of Holidays and Cultural Celebration. Shell Education. ISBN 978-1-4258-1048-1.

9. Belle, Karl Vadivella (2018).Thaipusam in Malaysia. ISEAS Yousuf Ishak Institute. ISBN 978-9-8147-8666-9.

10. Thaipusam 2022: From Date to History, Here is everything you need to know about the Tamil festival. First Post, January 18 2022.

11. 9. Geoff Teece (2005).Sikhism. Smart Apple Media.ISBN 978-1-58340-469-0.

12 Dhillon,Iqbal S. (1998). Folk Dances of Punjab. Delhi. National Bookshop.

13. Schreffler, Gibb. (2013). Situating Bhangra Dance: a critical introduction. South Asian History and Culture 4 (3): 364-412.

14. Abu Talib Ahmad (2014). Museums, history, and culture in Malaysia. NUS Press. ISBN 978-9971-69-855-3.

15. Muzium Negara. jmm.gov.my

Chapter 6

1. Ooi Keat Gin (2015). 'Disparate Identities: Penang from a Historical Perspective, 1780-1941. Kajian Malaysia 33(2): 27-52. ISSN 0127-4082.

2. Christie, Clive (1998). A Modern History of Southeast Asia: Decolonisation, Nationalism and Separatism. I.B.Tarus. ISBN 978-1-86064-354-5.

3. Ooi,Kee Beng (2012).'Penang before Francis Light (as the English saw it in 1905).' Penang Monthly.

4. Hockton, Keith (2012). Penang: An Inside Guide to its Historic Homes, Buildings, Monuments and Parks. Petaling Jaya. MPH Group. ISBN 978-967-415-303-8.

5. The Founding of Penang. www.sabrizain.org.

6. Light, Francis (The Light Letters). AIM25.Part of Malay Documents. School of Oriental and African Studies, London.

7. Pantai Cenang- Everything you Need to Know About Pantai Cenang. Langkawi-info-.com

8. Mohamed Zahir Haji Ismail (2000). The Legeneds of Langkawi. Utusan Publications and Distributors. ISBN 978-967-6110-275.

9. Berhad,Genting Malaysia. Resorts World Genting.www. rwgenting.com.

10. Winstedt,R O (1922). Two Legends of Mallaca. Journal of Straits Branch of the Royal Asiatic Society. 85:40.

11. Ravichandran Moorthy (2009).The Evolution of the Chitty Community of Malacca. Jebat Malaysian Journal of History, Politics and Strategic Studies. 36:1-15.

12. Malacca, a Dutch conquest forgotten (2015). MDDP.

13. Background of Johar Baru City Council and History of Johor Baru.Malaysian Digital Repository,

14. Federal Territory of Kuala Lumpur. Department of Statistics Malaysia.

15. J.M.Gullick 91983). The Story of Kuala Lumpur 1857-1939. Eastern Universities Press. ISBN 978-967-908-028-5.

16. Ziauddin Sardar (2000). The Consumption of Kuala Lumpur. Reaktion Books. ISBN 978-1-86189-057-3.

17. Seng Fatt Lam (2000). Insider's Kuala Lumpur. Times Books International. ISBN 978-981-204-876-9.

18. Destinations: Kuala Lumpur. Tourism Malaysia,2008.

19. Kuala Lumpur. Columbia Encyclopedia, Sixth Edition,2007.

20. Kuala Lumpur Culture and Heritage: Traditions, Races, People. Kuala Lumpur Hotels and Travel Guide,2008.

21. 1. Zainal Kling (1994). Malay Socioreligeous Practices and Rituals. UNESCO China Conference. http://en.unesco.org-silkroad.

Chapter 7

1. Mohamed Zahir Haji Ismail (2000). The Legeneds of Langkawi. Utusan Publications and Distributors. ISBN 978-967-6110-275.

2. Pantai Cenang- Everything you Need to Know About Pantai Cenang. Langkawi-info-.com

3.Thulaja, Naidu Ratnala (2018).Tanjong Rhu Road. Infopedia. Government of Singapore.

4. Peninsular Malaysia (2022). Travelfish.

Part-II

Chapter 1

1. Juan L Rodriguez-Flores, Khalid Fakhro, Francisco Agosto Perez et al. (2016). Indigenous Arabs are descendants of the earliest split from ancient Eurasian Populations. Genome Research 26(2): 151-162.

2. Cann RL, Stoneking M, Wilson AC.(1987). Mitochondrial DNA and human evolution. Nature 325:31-36.

3. Armitage SJ,Jasim SA,et al. (2011).The Southern route "out of Africa": evidence for an early expansion of modern humans into Arabia. Science 331:453-456.

4. Hoyland, Roberts G (2001). Arabia and the Arabs. Routledge. ISBN 0-203-76392-0.

4. Arab People (2023).Encyclopaedia Britannica October 3, 2023.

5. The Nomadic Tribes of Arabia. (2016). Boundless.com

6. Resto,Jan(2013). The Arabs in Antiquity: The History from the Assyrians to the Umayyads. Routledge. ISBN 978-1-136-87282-2.

7. Patai, Raphael. The Arab Mind. Charles Scribner's Sons, New York,1973.

8. Suwaed, Muhammad. (2015). Historical Dictionary of the Bedouins. Rowman and Littlefield Publishers. ISBN 9781442254510.

9. Habib Hassan Touma (1996). The Music of the Arabs. trans. Lourie Schwartz.Portland, Oregon: Amadeus Press. ISBN 0-931340-88-8.

10. Farmer, Henry George (1988). Historical Facts of the Arabian Musical Influence. Ayer Publishing. ISBN 0-405-08495.

11. Bounaventura, Wendy (2010).Serpent of the Nile: women and dance in the Arab world. London.Saqi. ISBN 978-0863566288.

12. Fraser, Kathleen W. (2014). Before they were Belly Dancers: European Accounts of Female Entertainers in Egypt 1760-1870. McFarland.ISBN 9780786494330.

13. Overview of Belly Dance: Egyptian Folkloric style belly dancing. www.atlantabellydance.com.

14. Hawthom, Ainsley (2019).Middle Eastern Dance and What We Call It.Dance Research. 37(1):1-17.

15. Al-Rawi,Rosina Fawzia (1999). Grandmother's Secrets: The Ancient Rituals and Healing Power of Belly Dancing.Interlink Books. ISBN 978-1-56656-302-4.

16. Martin, Andrew R; Mathew Mihalka Ph. D. (2020). Music Around the World: A Global Encyclopedia (3 volumes): A Global Encyclopedia. Abc-Clio. ISBN 9781610694995.

17. Dallal, Tamalyn (2004). Belly Dancing for Fitness. Berkeley: Ulysses Press. ISBN 9781569754108.

Chapter 2

1. Slot, B. (1991). The Origins of Kuwait. BRILL, P 110. ISBN 978-90-04-09409-3.
2. Britannica: History of Kuwait. www.Britannica.com
3. McGinley, Shane (2019). Born to Lead: Sheikh Mubarak Al Abdulah Al Mubarak Al Sabah. Arabian Business.
4. Kuwait Personality Profile. www.16personalities.com
5. Mohammed E. Al-Habib (2023). Kuwait's 'Ajam' merchants: a transnational community (1896-1950). Middle Eastern Studies 1-19. S2CID 265365149.
6. Mohammed E. Alhabib (2010). The Shia migration from Southwest Iran to Kuwait: Push-Pull factors during the Late Nineteenth and Early Twentieth centuries. (Thesis). Georgia State University.

Chapter 3

1. Saifi, A Quyum (1986). Kuwait University and its Evaluation program. Higher Education 15(5): 421-447. ISBN 0018-1560.
2. Kuwait University at the New University City at Shadadiyah. Pagethink.com

Chapter 4

1. Ahmad Hamada(2015). The Integeration History of Kuwaiti Television from 1957-1990: An Audience Generated Oral Narrative on the Arrival and Integeration of the Devices in the City—(Thesis) Virginia Commonwealth University.
2. Alhajri,Khalifah Rashed (2017). A Scenographer's Perspective on Arabic Theatre and Arab-Muslim Identity. (PhD Thesis) University of Leeds, UK.
3. Shooting the Past. (2013). y-oman.com
4. Hammond, Andrew, ed (2017).Pop Culture in North Africa and the Middle East Entertainment and Society Around the World. California. ABC-CLIO. ISBN 9781440833847.
5. Rolf Killius (2014). Hidden Treasure Reflections on Traditional Music in Kuwait. Qatar Digital Library.
6. Uaby, Laith. (2011). Performing the Past: Sea Music in the Arab Gulf States. BiblioBazzar. ISBN 9781244006607.
7. Sheikh Jaber Al Ahmad Cultural Centre.jacckw.com

8. Kuwait Museum of Modern Art. myartguides.com

9. Gonzales, Desi (2014).Acquiring Modernity: Kuwait at the 14th International Architecture Exhibition. Art Papers.

10.Exell,Karen(2016). Modernity and the Museum in the Arabian Peninsula. Taylor and Francis. ISBN 9781317279006.

11.Dar al-Athar al-Islamiyyah at Amricani Cultural Centre. darmuseum.org.kw

12. Muslim Occasions.(2023). In Wikipedia. http://simple. wikipedia.org

Chapter 5

1. Sciolino, Elaine (1991). The Outlaw State: Saddam Hussain's quest for power and the Gulf Crisis. John Wiley & Sons. ISBN 978-0-471-54299-5.

2. Stork Joe; Lesch,Ann M. (1990). Background to the Crisis. Why War? Middle East Report (167, November-December 1990). Middle East Research and Information Project (MERIP) 11-18. JSTOR 3012998.

3. Cooper Tom; Sadik Ahmad (2007). Iraqi Invasion of Kuwait, 1990. Air Combat Information Group Journal.

4. Simons, Geoff (2004). Iraq: from Sumer to Post-Saddam (3rd ed). Palgrave Macmillan. ISBN 978-1-4039-1770-6.

5. Finlan, Alastair (2003). The Gulf War 1991. Osprey. ISBN 978-1-84176-574-7.

6. Interogator Shares Saddam's Confessions. Absnews.com 24 January 2008.

7. Waldman, Shmuel (2005). Beyond a Reasonable Doubt. Feldheim Publishers, p179. ISBN 978-1-58330-806-6.

8. Royce, Knut (29 August 1990). MIDDLE EAST CRISIS Secret Offer Iraq Sent Pullout Deal to US. Newsday. New York.

9. Tyler, Patrick E. (3 January 1991). CONFRONTATION IN THE GULF; Arafat Eases Stand on Kuwait-Palestine Link. The New York Times. New York.

10. DESERT SHEILD AND DESERT STORM: A CHRONOLOGY AND TROOP LIST FOR THE 1990-1991 PERSIAN GULF CRISIS.9PDF). Apps. dtic.mil.

11. After the War Kuwait: Kuwait Emir, Tired and Tearful, Returns to His Devastated Land. New York Times, 15 Mar 1991.

12. The Massacre of Withdrawing Soldiers on "The Highway of Death." New York Commission hearing, May 11, 1991.
13. Yann Le Troquer, Rozennn Hommery al-Oudat (Spring 1999). From Kuwait to Jordan: The Palestinian's Third Exodus. Journal of Palestine Studies 28(3): 37-51. JSTOR 2538306.
14. Husain, T. (1995). Kuwait Oil Fires: Regional Environmental Perspectives. Oxford. BPC Wheatons Ltd.

Chapter 6.

1. Al-Jassar Mohammad Khalid A (2009). Constancy and Change in Contemporary Kuwait City. The Socio-Cultural Dimensions of the Kuwait Courtyard and Diwnniyya. (PhD thesis). The University of Wisconsin-Milwakee.
2. Bell, Gawain (1983). Shadows on the Sand: The Memoirs of Sir Gawain Bell. C. Hurst. ISBN 978-0-905838-92-2.
3. Farah Al-Nakib (2016). Kuwait Transformed: A History of Oil and Urban Life. Stanford University Press.
4. Crystal, Jill (1994). Kuwait Constitution. In Metz, Helen Chapin (ed). Persian Gulf States: country studies (3rd ed). Federal Research Division, Library of Congress. ISBN 0-8444-0793-3.
5. Paul Salem (2007).Kuwait: Politics in a Participatory Emirate. Carnegie Endowment for International Peace (3):4. JSTOR resrep12897.

Chapter 7

1, Kuwait has an ambitious plan to tame sand and dust storms. WIRED Middle East.Sci ence. Oct 2023.
2. Galindo Michelle (2009). Chalet Architecture and Design. Braun Architecture AG. ISBN 3-03768-021-0.
3.Heialy,Yasmin Al (2016). Kuwait's Multi-Billion Sea City will be ready in 25 years. Costructionweekonline.com
4. Jones, D. A., Nithyanandan, M., Williams I. (2012). Sabah Al-Ahmad Sea City Kuwait: development of a sustainable man-made coastal ecosystem in a saline desert.Aquatic Ecosystem Health & Management. 15: 84-92.

Part-III
Chapter I

1. al-Idrisi, *Opus Georgraphicum* (ed), Bombaci, A., Rizzitano, U., Rubinacci,R., and Veccia Vaglieri, L., Naples,Rome, 1972.
2. al Idrisi, trans. Into French From the Arabic, Jaubert, P. A. La Geographie d' Edrisi, Paris (1836).
3. Bahrain Etymology, History, Geography, Government and Politics. The Free Encyclopedia. rsmag.org.
4. Arabia and the Arabs: From the Bronze Age to the Coming of Islam. Routledge, p 28. ISBN 978-0-415-19535-5.
5. McCoy, Eric Andrew (2008). Iranians in Bahrain and the United Arab Emirates: Migration, Minorities and Identities in the Persian Gulf Arab States. p 73. ISBN 978-0-549-93507-0.
6. Hamza, Abdul Aziz (2009). Tears on an Island: History of Diasters in the Kingdom of Bahrain. Al Waad. p. 165. ISBN 978-99901-92-22-3.
7. David Pollock (2017). Sunnis and Shia in Bahrain: New Survey Shows Both Conflicts and Consensus. Fikra Forum. Washington Institute for Near East Policy.
8. Fattouh, Mayssa (2009). Bahrain's Art and Culture Scenes. Nafas.
9. Meixler, Louis (20 September 1998). An Ancient Garden of Eden is Unearthed in the Persian Gulf's Bahrain. Los Angeles Times.

Chapter 2

1. Palm Jumeirah- History, Description and Facts. Britannica. www.britannica.com
2. Religion in Dubai (2010). Wayback Machine. Dubaidreams.
3. "Dubai remains one Of The World's most visited cities. Mastercard Global Destination Cities Index 2019.
4. McCarthy, Niall (2021). The Cities with the Most Five-Star Hotels. (infographic)." Forbes.
5. Winkler, Mthew A (2018).Dubai is the Very Model of a Modern Mideast Economy. Bloomberg.
6. Dubai (city) I Geography, Creek & History. Britannica. 2024. www.britannica.com
7. Ibrahim Al Abed, Peter Hellyer (2001). United Arab Emirate: A Perspective. Trident Press. ISBN 978-1-900-724-47-0.

8. Krane, Jim (2010). Dubai. The Story of the World's Fastest City. London.England: Atlantic. ISBN 978-1-84887-009-3.

9. Al Maktoum, Mohammed bin Rashid (2012).Spirit of the Union. UAE. Motivate. ISBN 978-1-86063-330-0.

10. Sampler & Eigner (2008). Sand to Silicon.Going Global, UAE. Motivate. ISBN 978-1-86063-254-9.

Chapter 3

1. Allen, Calvin H. (1981). The Indian Merchant Community of Masqat. Bulletin of the School of Oriental and African Studies 44(1): 39-53. ISSN 0041-977X.

2. Museums. 2009. Omanet.com

3. Common, Richard K. (2018). Barriers to Developing Leadership in The Sultanate of Oman. International Journal of Leadership Studies.

4. Romey, Kristin (2016). Shipwreck Discovered from Explorer Vasco da Gama's Fleet. National Geographic March 16, 2016.

5. Peterson, J. E. (2007). Chronology. Historical Muscat. Brill. P. 117+ ISBN 978-90-04-15266-3.

6. Paige Peterson (May 3, 2016). Oman: The Pearl of Arabia. National Council on US-Arab Relations.

7. Darke, Diane (2010). Oman: The Brad Travel Guide. Brad Travel Guides. ISBN 978-184-16233-20.

ACKNOWLEDGEMENTS

Professor Abdullatif Al-Bader edited the book's text. Professor Hussain Dashti contributed some pictures to the text from his vast collection of images of Kuwait and the Arabian Gulf Countries. Mr Harris Perriera took live photos of the Kuwaiti desert and the people living there, which are included in the text. Mr Palvinder Mahal, Graphic Designer, advised on the images and text pictures. Advocates Meghna Arora and Manjit Singh prepared a comprehensive report on different copyright laws, particularly the Indian laws, and their compatibility with the creative common licenses of Wikimedia permitting the free use of copyrighted pictures, including commercial use, after fulfilling specific requirements.

ABOUT THE AUTHOR

Professor Jasbir S. Juggi, 89, obtained his medical and doctoral (PhD) qualifications from leading Universities in India in the fifties and sixties of the last century. He started his first level of academic teaching and research career in medical physiology in India. He left India in 1968 to take up senior academic positions at the University of Malaya, Kuala Lumpur, Malaysia, and later at the Faculty of Medicine, Kuwait University, Kuwait, where he retired as Chairman and Academic Vice-Dean of the faculty in 2006. He has published extensively in medical science and attended numerous international conferences and meetings where he presented his research and gave invited lectures.

Throughout his medical career, he has never forgotten his early obsession with history and reading real-life stories and events. While in Malaysia and later in Kuwait, he studied and absorbed the culture and lifestyles of the people of these two diverse countries, separated by hundreds of miles. These experiences are elaborated in the text of the book: "Ends Apart: Malaysia and Kuwait."

After his final retirement in 2016 from an active academic career of more than fifty years, Professor Juggi established his retirement home in Gurgaon, India, where he spends time reminiscing his past life, not always happy and sometimes full of recriminations and regrets.

9 798894 753409